Cambridge Elements

Elements in the Philosophy of Biology
edited by
Grant Ramsey
KU Leuven

MODELLING EVOLUTION

Walter Veit
*University of Reading and
Ludwig-Maximilians-Universität München*

Shaftesbury Road, Cambridge CB2 8EA, United Kingdom

One Liberty Plaza, 20th Floor, New York, NY 10006, USA

477 Williamstown Road, Port Melbourne, VIC 3207, Australia

314–321, 3rd Floor, Plot 3, Splendor Forum, Jasola District Centre, New Delhi – 110025, India

103 Penang Road, #05-06/07, Visioncrest Commercial, Singapore 238467

Cambridge University Press is part of Cambridge University Press & Assessment, a department of the University of Cambridge.

We share the University's mission to contribute to society through the pursuit of education, learning and research at the highest international levels of excellence.

www.cambridge.org
Information on this title: www.cambridge.org/9781009459976

DOI: 10.1017/9781009459983

© Walter Veit 2025

This publication is in copyright. Subject to statutory exception and to the provisions of relevant collective licensing agreements, no reproduction of any part may take place without the written permission of Cambridge University Press & Assessment.

When citing this work, please include a reference to the DOI 10.1017/9781009459983

First published 2025

A catalogue record for this publication is available from the British Library

ISBN 978-1-009-45999-0 Hardback
ISBN 978-1-009-45997-6 Paperback
ISSN 2515-1126 (online)
ISSN 2515-1118 (print)

Cambridge University Press & Assessment has no responsibility for the persistence or accuracy of URLs for external or third-party internet websites referred to in this publication and does not guarantee that any content on such websites is, or will remain, accurate or appropriate.

For EU product safety concerns, contact us at Calle de José Abascal, 56, 1°, 28003 Madrid, Spain, or email eugpsr@cambridge.org

Modelling Evolution

Elements in the Philosophy of Biology

DOI: 10.1017/9781009459983
First published online: September 2025

Walter Veit
University of Reading and Ludwig-Maximilians-Universität München
Author for correspondence: Walter Veit, wrwveit@gmail.com

Abstract: This Element discusses the central role of models within evolutionary biology, offering an accessible introduction and synthesis of literature in both evolutionary biology and the philosophy of models. We will examine three questions: first, what does it mean to be a 'model' and to engage in 'modelling'? Second, what types of models are employed within evolutionary biology? Third, how can models of evolution be tested? In exploring the answers to these questions, this Element hopes to highlight how evolutionary biology and philosophy of biology can usefully interact to understand conceptual and methodological problems arising from modelling evolution.

Keywords: modelling; evolutionary biology; idealization; scientific representations; model-based science

© Walter Veit 2025

ISBNs: 9781009459990 (HB), 9781009459976 (PB), 9781009459983 (OC)
ISSNs: 2515-1126 (online), 2515-1118 (print)

Contents

1 Introduction	1
2 What Does It Mean to 'Model' Evolution?	3
3 Types of Models in Evolutionary Biology	14
4 Testing Models of Evolution	35
5 Conclusion and Further Discussion	49
References	52

1 Introduction

Evolutionary biology is a historical science with the goal of understanding the origin and diversity of life. Evolutionary biologists have developed a vast range of diverse and ingenious models to achieve this. The goal of this Element is to understand why and how models are used in evolutionary biology.

Before we begin, however, let me express a note of caution to any scientists or students of evolutionary biology who are reading this Element: This is not a practical guide for aspiring modellers on how to model evolution. It is a text in the *philosophy of biology* that addresses some of the deeper methodological and conceptual questions regarding an aspect of evolutionary biology that most scientists remain silent about. These questions include:

- What *are* models?
- What does it *mean* to model evolution?
- What *types* of models are there?
- How can models of evolution be *tested*?
- How do different types of models *interact* with each other to advance our understanding of evolution?

These are, of course, questions any scientist engaged in the process of modelling evolution should think about, but they are rarely given space to examine in depth. This Element, while short, is an attempt to examine these questions in an accessible, yet rigorous manner that goes beyond a mere survey of the existing literature.

A central, if not *the* central, activity in science is the construction of models to represent real-world phenomena. It is unsurprising, then, that the philosophy of models/modelling has grown into a substantial subfield within the philosophy of science, with numerous articles published in this area every year. Similarly, the theory of evolution, owing to its foundational role in the biological sciences, has long been the core focus for philosophers of biology. Yet despite the extensive attention both topics have received from philosophers of science, comparatively little work bridges these fields to deepen our understanding of how evolutionary processes are modelled.

I am, of course, not denying that there are important exceptions to this trend, which I will discuss throughout this Element. Rather, my point is that one would expect a much broader philosophical literature combining insights from these two fields to deepen our understanding of how evolution has been represented. Indeed, even my own work has not typically performed this integration. While I have written articles in the philosophy of (evolutionary) biology and the philosophy of models, and even spent time in the labs of evolutionary biologists, relatively few of my own articles have directly focussed on how models are used within evolutionary biology. Most modellers that I spoke with had never even read a paper in the philosophy of models, leaving me with the sense that there is an unsatisfied need for an accessible synthesis of research across these fields. The goal of this Element, then, is to overcome what I consider to be a neglect of attention paid by philosophers of modelling, philosophers of biology, and even evolutionary biologists themselves to the importance of the philosophy of modelling evolution.

Finally, let me say something about my intended audience. This Element is targeted at philosophers of modelling, philosophers of biology, evolutionary biologists, and anyone interested in how models contribute to our understanding of evolution (and to some extent science more generally). Since the Cambridge Elements in the philosophy of biology are meant to offer a hybrid between a concise and well-organized introduction to important subjects and the original and unique views of their authors, I will not assume any prior knowledge in the three areas synthesized in this Element: that is, (i) the philosophy of (evolutionary) biology, (ii) the philosophy of modelling, and (iii) evolutionary biology. Each of the target audiences of this Element is likely to be unfamiliar with at least one of these areas, making it useful to explain each concept and method as I go, without excessive jargon. My hope is that I have succeeded in making this Element accessible and useful to a diverse readership, less dry and more engaging than a standard introductory text, and with the potential to inspire further integration between these fields and future collaboration between researchers.

For *philosophers of modelling*, evolutionary biology offers an incredibly rich and diverse set of models to draw on as case studies to understand how models work and the roles of modelling within science. For *philosophers of biology*, this Element will offer a strong case for the thesis that evolutionary biology can only be understood through the models and modelling-practices employed by scientists. Finally, for *evolutionary biologists*, this Element will invite them to reflect on their own methodology and how different types of models can help them in the pursuit of knowledge about the process of evolution.

With this introduction out of the way, let me offer a brief outline for the rest of this Element.

1.1 Outline

This Element is structured as follows. Section 2 explores the conceptual question of what 'models' are and what it means to be engaged in 'modelling'. Section 3 examines the different types of models that can be used to model evolution. Section 4 investigates the problem of how such models can be tested. Finally, Section 5 concludes this Element by offering a summary of the arguments advanced in this work and proposes further directions for future research in this area.

2 What Does It Mean to 'Model' Evolution?

When writing about the philosophy of modelling and models of evolution, an inevitable conceptual question arises: What is meant by the terms 'model' and 'modelling'? Biologists and philosophers of biology may hope for a straightforward answer to this question, but the meanings of these terms are highly contested within the philosophy of models. Colloquially, as well as among researchers in biology and philosophy, these terms are often taken as a shorthand for referring to mathematical entities and activities. This is, of course, hardly surprising given their ubiquity in both science generally and evolutionary biology specifically. If you open any textbook on evolution, it will be clear that much, if not most, contemporary work in evolutionary biology involves models of this type. Anyone training to become an evolutionary biologist today will inevitably encounter mathematical models. Prestigious journals such as *Nature Ecology & Evolution*, *The American Naturalist*, *Evolution Letters*, *Ecology and Evolution*, *Journal of Evolutionary Biology*, or even *Evolution* are filled with articles featuring such formal models of evolution. Yet this was not always the norm.

The work of Charles Darwin (1859) in *The Origin of Species* is an excellent case in point showing that evolutionary biology, at least originally, did not involve the kind of mathematical and highly idealized model-building we associate with much of the work going on in the field today. Indeed, some philosophers working in both the philosophy of models and the philosophy of evolutionary biology, such as Peter Godfrey-Smith (2007), have argued that Darwin's work contained no models at all. But this is a mistake. While Darwin's work didn't contain mathematical models, it is filled with informal written models that later inspired biologists to create more precise formal mathematical models, as well as simulations (Thomson, 2017).

We can thus begin this philosophical analysis by making a distinction between formal and informal models in evolutionary biology. Formal models include mathematical models, computational models, and statistical models. Informal models can be written, verbal, pictorial, and even mental. As cognitive scientists have demonstrated over the last decades, much of how we operate in the world is based on mental models. Thus, for any reader of this Element, there will be a mental model of how they understand evolution to work, which may be more or less accurate, given how widespread misunderstandings about evolution are among not only students but also instructors (Abenes & Caballes, 2020; De Santis, 2021; Gregory, 2009; Nehm & Reilly, 2007; Nelson, 2008).

But before we discuss the diversity of models that evolutionary biologists use to advance our understanding of evolutionary processes in Section 3, we need to answer the question of what 'models' are and what it means to 'model'. Clearly, we cannot just refer to mathematical entities and activities if models can also be informal. But ostensive definitions (i.e. definition by pointing out examples) that merely list a variety of models or model types are also not sufficient, since they provide us with no deeper conceptual understanding of the general category. However, is there anything that unifies entities that can range so widely? Can we offer a definition of these terms by identifying necessary and sufficient conditions that capture the essences of 'models' and 'modelling'? Some philosophers, such as Nelson Goodman, have expressed scepticism about this question:

> Few terms are used in popular and scientific discourse more promiscuously than 'model'. A model is something to be admired or emulated, a pattern, a case in point, a type, a prototype, a specimen, a mock-up, a mathematical description – almost anything from a naked blonde to a quadratic equation – and may bear to what it models almost any relation of symbolization. (Nelson Goodman, 1976, p. 171)

Given this, there appears to be nothing inherent to the properties of those entities called 'models' that makes them models. Philosophers might call this the ontology of models (i.e. their metaphysical structure of reality similar to how H_2O = water). Instead, philosophers have largely tried to define 'models' in terms of their function or purpose in science. But what could this function be?

While the philosophy of models literature is full of disagreements and the recognition of a wide range of potential functions for models, there is one answer to this question that has come closest to achieving something resembling consensus, and that is: the function is to *represent* (Downes, 2020; Odenbaugh, 2018; Teller, 2001). An early expression of this idea came from Hughes who argued that the 'characteristic – perhaps the only characteristic – that all theoretical models have in common is that they provide representations of parts of the world, or of the world as we describe it' (Hughes, 1997, p. S325). With the proliferation of new model types and the ever-expanding range of modelling approaches proposed by philosophers (far too many to discuss comprehensively here), it has become even more common to think that only the notion of representation can unify this diverse literature. As Downes puts it: 'There is almost complete consensus among philosophers of science working on models on only one idea: models are representations or models represent' (Downes, 2020, p. 52).

This prevalent usage also reflects ordinary usage of the term 'model'. The *Oxford English Dictionary*, for instance, offers the following definition of the term 'model': 'A representation of structure, and related senses' (Oxford English Dictionary, 2024). Similarly, the *Encyclopædia Britannica* defines 'scientific modelling' as the 'generation of a physical, conceptual, or mathematical representation of a real phenomenon' (Rogers, 2023). Accordingly, let me offer a first tentative definition of the central terms of this Element as follows:

Models: To be a scientific model is to be a scientific representation.
Modelling: To engage in scientific modelling is to construct scientific models.

With these definitions in place, let us now turn towards the new philosophical problem of how to understand the concept of 'representation' that underlies the understanding of models and modelling.

2.1 Models as Representations

Modellers often talk about using their models to *represent* some phenomenon, but what does that actually amount to? Reflecting the difficulty of working this idea out in detail, there is now a fairly large philosophical literature on the 'models as representations' view (see Frigg & Nguyen, 2017 for an overview). Hughes, whom I mentioned before as a defender of a representationalist view, himself admits that 'the concept of representation is as slippery as that of a model' (Hughes, 1997, p. S325). But while there is ongoing disagreement over how models achieve their representational purpose, there is broad agreement that representations require both a *target* phenomenon to represent and a specific *purpose* for which the representations are put to use. Let us now examine both of these ideas in order to understand the models-as-representations view better.

What is a model *target*? The target of a model is typically a mechanism or process that scientists aim to understand better, but which is difficult or impossible to investigate directly. This scenario is often the case in evolutionary biology. Since evolutionary processes often unfold over timescales far exceeding the lifespans of scientists, models become indispensable tools for advancing our understanding of evolutionary biology. I say 'often' rather than 'always', because microbiology provides an important exception to this trend. As we were able to observe during the COVID-19 pandemic, the SARS-CoV-2 kept (and still keeps) evolving new strains that made it more resistant to vaccines, putting the idea of evolvability into public discourse. Mathematical models predicting the likely evolution of new strains were common during the pandemic (Yagan et al., 2021) and nicely reflect how evolutionary biologists are not just interested in modelling the past. Similarly, microbial populations in laboratories receive a lot of attention from evolutionary biologists since they allow us to observe evolution in real time (O'Malley et al., 2015). Indeed, as I shall argue in Section 3, such microbial populations can constitute experimental models or so-called 'model organisms' (though I prefer the 'model populations' since the target isn't individuals) to represent more general evolutionary dynamics. But microbiology is not the only area where we evolutionary biologists study non-geological timescales of evolution. In the twenty-first century, evolutionary biology gradually shifted towards a recognition of evolution even within our own timescales, studying rapid evolutionary changes even in single generations, often due to events such as climate change (Aguirre-Liguori et al., 2021).

What is the *representational relationship* between such models and their targets? One of the most intuitive views in the literature spells out this connection in terms of similarity or resemblance between models and their targets (Giere, 1988; Weisberg, 2013). A successful model or representation is then one that shares enough similarity (or rather, relevant similarities) with its target to be used as a placeholder or surrogate system that can be studied in its stead. While a simple mathematical model may be strikingly different from the complex biological phenomenon it is trying to represent, what matters is that the relevant properties are captured in the variables of the model (e.g. mutation rate, survival chance, and reproductive output in an evolutionary model), to be useful to the modeller. Indeed, some models in evolutionary biology are incredibly simple, representing only a few key aspects of the target.

Let us look at one of the best examples to illustrate this point: John Maynard Smith and George R. Price's Hawk–Dove Model, that pioneered the field of evolutionary game theory (Maynard Smith & Price, 1973). Imagine a population in which individuals have an interest in procuring a territory, which yields a fitness payoff of V if they do. When two

Table 1 A payoff matrix for the Hawk–Dove Game

	Hawk	Dove
Hawk	$(V-C)/2, (V-C)/2$	$V, 0$
Dove	$0, V$	$V/2, V/2$

individuals meet, they have a choice between acting aggressively (the hawk strategy) or passively (the dove strategy) as shown in Table 1.

If both individuals are aggressive they split the territory but have to pay a fitness cost C for the fight (e.g. injury or energy loss from the fight). If both are passive they split the territory without having to pay that cost. If a hawk meets a dove, however, the entire territory goes to the aggressive individual. Where would evolution lead such a population of hawks and doves? Maynard Smith and Price (1973) proposed the solution through the concept of an evolutionarily stable strategy (ESS). They define an ESS as follows: If an incumbent strategy i is an ESS, then there cannot be another invading strategy/mutant m whose fitness u is higher such that it would increase its proportion in the population. If the payoff of an incumbent is equal to that of a mutant, mutants must do worse when they play against each other than if an incumbent plays against a mutant. This would allow the incumbent to take over a mutant population. This can be represented as follows:

$$U(i) > U(m)$$

Or

$$U(i,i) = U(m,i) \text{ and } U(i,m) > U(m,m)$$

If $V > C$, hawk becomes the dominant strategy, but if $C > V$, there will be a mixed population of hawks and doves (or individuals will themselves mix their strategy) because a population of pure doves or hawks could always be invaded by the other. We will look at this model in more detail in Section 4, but we can see here that this simple idealized model nicely illustrates why resource conflicts in nature persist but are typically resolved with minor complications. Furthermore, the model helps to illustrate the general importance of frequency dependence in the evolution of traits in a population. This model is useful despite leaving out many features of the environment, which is not uncommon in evolutionary models. As Neto et al. observe, environmental features in evolutionary models are often 'highly idealized or abstracted away. If they are included in mathematical models they are typically subsumed within a single fitness coefficient' (Neto et al., 2023, p. 18). What matters, despite all these idealizations and omissions of features of real target systems, is that our model is similar enough to the targets being represented to yield explanatory insights.

One of the reasons why the similarity account has gained popularity is that it accounts for misrepresentation. While models are typically designed to be faithful to their target systems, they are also full of idealizations and omissions, sparking extensive debate about how falsehoods in models can play useful roles rather than always being negative. Potochnik (2017), for instance, has argued that 'idealizations aid in representation not simply by what they eliminate, such as noise or non-central influences, but in virtue of what they add, that is, their positive representational content' (p. 50). Indeed, a perfectly faithful model with complete similarity could only be the target itself, which would make the testing of models irrelevant and the model more generally pointless.

Here philosophers of science often use the analogy of a map offering a model of a city, subway network, or hiking paths (Nguyen & Frigg, 2022). Maps necessarily idealize to be useful. A one-to-one mirroring would be too complex to be usable, which is why we need to think about *fit-for-purpose*. The same applies to the use of maps within evolutionary biology, which I shall discuss in Section 3. What matters for models then is not whether or not they are true, which isn't even a question that can be answered, but rather whether they are *useful*. Indeed, this leads us to another crucial issue: the purposes of models.

2.2 The Purposes of Models

What is a model's *purpose*? In order to evaluate whether a model is useful, good, or successful, we must determine the purpose for which it is put to use. As Wendy Parker argues, we need an 'adequacy-for-purpose view' of models, where they are evaluated not on how accurate their representations are, but whether they succeed in what they have been built for (Parker, 2020, p. 457). We will return to this idea in Section 4 where we'll examine how models in evolutionary biology can be tested. Let us start now by asking: what is the goal of the modeller? Depending on what goal one has in mind for a model, it will achieve its representational function in different ways. What makes something a relevant similarity between model and target will come from the purpose we have for that model. Importantly, the goals of models can vary radically.

Probably the first function many will think of is explanation. Models in evolutionary biology can explain why certain patterns or traits evolved and under which conditions they did so. In doing so, models make assumptions about their target system that allow us to reason about the system, which is why one often hears the phrase *model-based reasoning* in discussions about the role of models. In principle this could enable evolutionary biologists to reason about evolutionary processes in the abstract, without any direct target. This is sometimes described as *targetless modelling* or the modelling of a fictional system, such as a population with three or four sexes (Frigg & Nguyen, 2016, 2021).

Indeed, some philosophers have argued for the importance of the so-called exploratory models that help scientists to explore potential scenarios without having to intervene in the target system itself (Gelfert, 2019; Massimi, 2019). This is especially true for mathematical models, where assumptions and parameters can easily be changed due to the more abstract representations of the target. Such counterfactual reasoning can help us to understand, for example, why certain traits did not evolve, for example.

While models in evolutionary biology are typically concerned with the past, as I have already mentioned, how evolutionary biologists sometimes also use their models to predict the future, such as the evolvability of new strains of viruses. With climate change constituting a threat to many species, evolutionary biologists are now becoming more interested in offering predictions for the extinction of species or adaptations species may undergo (Chown et al., 2010; Munday et al., 2013; Pau et al., 2011; Waldvogel et al., 2020; Wortel et al., 2023). This has made models in evolutionary biology much more future oriented than it used to be, but this has not yet entered into the public perception of the field.

Another purpose of many models is to directly represent or convey important (and often complex) information condensed into a simpler form. Since humans are visual creatures, many such models take the form of diagrams, such as tree of life models, which ease the communication and understanding of ideas and information. I will discuss these models in more detail in Section 3. Many of these models also have an educational function and are often found in textbooks, such as phylogenetic trees to represent the relationships of different species.

Finally, modellers often also aim at intervention to study causation. When real-world systems cannot be intervened on (e.g. most evolutionary systems are too slow to study in the real world), models can illuminate the possible effects of intervention. For example, microbiologists frequently design experimental setups that are meant to model evolutionary processes in the real world and which allow for causal intervention, to determine processes of cause and effect. I will also discuss these in more detail in Section 3.

This list is far from exhaustive (see Frigg, 2022), but offers an elegant illustration of the great variety of purposes models may have. Notably, many of these goals need not conflict with each other and a single model can be used for multiple ends. Even when they do conflict, modellers may nevertheless be interested in building a model that at least partially satisfies several goals that may trade-off against each other. Rather than just thinking about a single goal/purpose a model is designed for it is therefore often more useful to think about a set of goals for which a model is designed.

Based on this consideration of the purposes of models, we can thus amend our tentative definition of the terms 'models' and 'modelling' as follows:

Models: To be a scientific model is to represent a target for a scientific goal or set of goals.

Modelling: To engage in scientific modelling is to construct representations of a target for a scientific goal or set of goals.

These definitions offer valuable insights to anyone wondering about how models work and what they are – be they philosophers of science or practicing scientists. When examining what makes for a good model, or how to improve one, we can now explicitly ask: (i) what the purpose is for which our model is meant to be used/designed? as well as (ii) whether it has relevant similarities with its target system? However, philosophical inquiry rarely just settles on a single solution – as wonderful as that may be! Before we move on to discuss the different types of models employed in evolutionary biology, let me first offer a challenge to the representationalist view of models.

2.3 Challenges to the Representationalist Consensus

So far, I have presented and defended a representationalist view of models and modelling activities. Yet this view can be challenged. Although the representationalist view of models is widely shared, in recent years it has come under increasing fire. In this subsection, I will examine these arguments and ultimately defend a weaker version of the representationalism according to which many models in evolutionary biology have the role of presentation, but not all.

Ironically, I find myself here in an odd position, as I have myself previously argued not only that the consensus view of models as representations is mistaken, but also that no alternative account can succeed in its place. I called this position 'model anarchism', to capture the spirit of Paul Feyerabend's critical view of philosophers' attempts to offer a unified analysis of science while neglecting its diversity. This position can be summarized in a single sentence.

Model Anarchism: 'models', 'modeling-practices', and 'model-based science' are too diverse, too context-sensitive, and serve too many scientific purposes and roles, as to constitute unified kinds that would allow for useful epistemic and ontologi[cal] analyses. (Veit, 2023, p. 226)

If this view is correct, one may wonder what the point would be of an Element that sought to inspire a thriving literature in the philosophy of models of evolution. I will therefore take this opportunity to critically examine my own arguments before ultimately demonstrating why they need not constitute a threat to the goals of this Element.

Earlier in this section, I emphasized that models are so diverse – and of so many different types (see discussion in Section 3) – that the only commonality to tie them together that has been accepted in the literature is the notion of representation. But this representationalist account of models can be regarded as both too broad and too narrow (Veit, 2023, p. 226). We will look at the argument for each of these in turn.

Firstly, the account can be challenged as being too broad because it fails to demarcate a unique scientific category. As Callender and Cohen (2006) have argued in this debate, there is no unique sense of representation within science. This makes it puzzling as to why there has been relatively little engagement from philosophers of science with the larger philosophical literature on representation. Indeed, I have recently argued elsewhere that philosophers have still paid too little attention to the similarities between representations within science and the arts (Veit & Milan, 2021). Without such a fundamental demarcation between scientific and other kinds of representation, however, it becomes less convincing that we can understand the special epistemic (i.e. knowledge-generating) roles of models within science simply by understanding representations.

The broader we stretch and deflate the concept of model to capture as many instances as possible of scientists' use of the term, the less clear it is that such a highly abstract account could be informative and useful. As I've outlined above, the notion of 'representation' is hardly more precise than that of 'model'. Many accounts have been proposed but there is little agreement on how we should understand representations. Much work in this field 'begins with the assumption that there is a single relationship that bears between models and the world' (O'Connor & Weatherall, 2016, p. 626), such as similarity or isomorphism (i.e. structure-preserving identity between model and target), but it is questionable that such a reductive account can succeed. The diversity of alternative views may simply capture genuine differences or multiplicities of ways in which models can be related to their targets.

Representationalist views in philosophy have also faced more general criticisms in the philosophy of mind (see for instance Myin & Hutto, 2015). This work has been used to argue that the representationalist account of models is by extension also 'untenable and unnecessary, a philosophical dead end' (de Oliveira, 2021, p. 209). While we need not go so far, the promises of the representationalist account of models – to resolve the philosophical puzzles about how models work, explain, and succeed in science – have not materialized. The view is too deflationary, without any meaningful commitments to how these representations are meant to be realized. If anything at all can be a model, it seems that the success of models within science becomes more philosophically puzzling rather than less so. As I argued in my original article:

> If almost every thing in science gets to count as a model and almost every activity can potentially be seen as modeling, the deflationary view may succeed in capturing all of MMM [models, modelling practices, and model-based science], but the account must ultimately be hollow and uninformative at such a level of abstraction – no less so than the commonly to Thales' attributed assertion that everything is water. (Veit, 2023, p. 233)

Indeed, the view becomes even more problematic when it fails to capture even those things that are purported to be models, as we shall now examine.

Secondly, the representationalist view can be challenged as being too narrow by showing that there are models that play important roles in science without any representational function. As Downes has perhaps most forcefully argued over the years, 'the role of models in science is by no means exhausted by representation' with there being 'far more expansive epistemic role[s] that models can play in forwarding scientific work' (Downes, 2011, p. 760). As the philosophical literature on models grows, more and more of these epistemic roles are uncovered. A now popular distinction in the literature between 'models of' a target system and 'models for' intervention provides a nice example (Downes, 2020; Keller, 2000; Ratti, 2020). While interventionist models are admittedly less common in evolutionary biology, the experimental models in microbiology I mentioned above can be understood as such models. As I will illustrate in Section 3, an evolutionary biologist could be seen as intervening in the evolutionary process itself, rather than as trying to represent evolution in a different system, thus blurring the boundary between model and experiment. Such models are deliberately designed for the purpose of interventions, rather than to merely represent a target.

The crux here seems to be a dependence on the goals of the biologist. Are they trying to understand a different system through the means of what is sometimes called a surrogate (or replacement) system, acting in place of some other target (Bolker, 2009; Mäki, 2009), or are they trying to more specifically understand evolution in this bacterial population and how it can be influenced? The single use of the term 'model' by Darwin in *On the Origin of Species* comes closer to this latter understanding: 'Breeders habitually speak of an animal's organisation as something quite plastic, which they can model almost as they please' (Darwin, 1859, p. 31). Here the word 'model' is used analogously to how one might model clay into desirable shapes. While it may be possible to detect some representational relationships in models built for interventions, the reduction of all models to their representational roles is bound to obstruct crucial differences between the things we call models. Indeed, with such vastly different usages of the term 'model' it becomes less clear that scientists are even trying to capture a unique form of scientific activity when they use the word.

Perhaps there is no account that could capture the diversity of different kinds of models. This sentiment has been forcefully expressed by O'Connor and Weatherall, who note that: 'The term ["]modeling,["] much like the term ["]science,["] picks out a set of practices that do not constitute any sort of natural category' (O'Connor & Weatherall, 2016, p. 614). Frigg has also recently expressed such scepticism after working within the representationalist framework of models for a long time:

> [N]either representation *tout court* nor inaccurate or indirect representation offer a general functional definition of models. This is not a proof that there is no functional definition of models. There could, in principle, be a different functional definition, one not couched in terms of representation, that captures all these activities under one large umbrella. However, the variety of models we encounter in scientific practice makes such a project look rather hopeless. (Frigg, 2022, p. 396)

Future work may well find a unifying umbrella under which to put all models and modelling activities, but it has not been found yet. I contend that we can leave this issue unresolved for the time being. We do not need to decide whether model anarchism is correct in order to agree that the representationalist account and definition of models offers a highly useful and often accurate conceptualization (dare I say, model) for thinking about the roles of models (see Veit, 2023 for a more extensive discussion of model anarchism). This is even more true within evolutionary biology, where non-representational purposes are typically rarer compared to other sciences. But it is good to keep in mind that these other purposes exist and that we should remain vigilant not to overgeneralize from the use of models in one area of evolutionary biology to another. We will explore many of these additional roles in the coming sections of this Element.

To conclude, philosophers have mounted powerful challenges to the representationalist consensus, though we were only able to scratch the surface of this debate here. The important takeaway from this section as a whole is that models in evolutionary biology serve important functions (most often of a representational kind) and that we need to think about the goals for which these models are intended in order to evaluate them.

2.4 Summary

The goal of this section was to answer the questions of what 'models' are and what it means to 'model' evolution. While newcomers to these debates may have hoped for a quick and easy resolution to these questions, in this rough overview of the literature on these terms I hope to have successfully shown that this debate is far from settled and deserves more attention than I was able to give it here. Nevertheless, there are several key insights and takeaways.

Firstly, models in evolutionary biology are typically *representations* of a target. For evolutionary biology, these targets will typically be real or imagined counterfactual populations. While the representationalist view may not always apply, it nonetheless remains a good starting point. As I have tried to emphasize in this section, in order to understand the roles of models within science we will need to pay special attention to the goals for which they are put to use. There is no independent sense of model evaluation to be had and Section 4 will be dedicated to discussing how best to test models of evolution. Unfortunately, this Element will not settle the question of what models are once-and-for-all. But instead of trying to find a general account of models, we can simply turn to the perhaps less ambitious, but scientifically more grounded approach of trying to understand the philosophical particularities of different types of models within evolutionary biology. This is the task to which we shall now turn.

3 Types of Models in Evolutionary Biology

At the beginning of this Element, I lamented the unexplored potential for further engagement between the philosophy of models and the philosophy of evolutionary biology. That there is this gap in the literature is unfortunate, precisely because few scientific theories have employed such a diversity of representationalist devices as the theory of evolution by natural selection. While mathematical models of evolution have admittedly received plenty of attention by philosophers, there are many different types of models employed by evolutionary biologists, and it is in their unique functions that we can best understand the scientific toolkit of evolutionary biology. Most of the literature on philosophy of models focusses on formal models, mathematical, computational, and statistical, but this focus may be misguided and reflect mistaken ideas about the inevitable replacement of informal models (e.g. thought experiments) by informal ones. As the Harvard biologist Jeremy Gunawardena notes:

> Informal models pervade biology. They help to guide our thinking, and experimentalists rely on them to design experiments. The model may turn out to be nonsense, and an experiment may reveal that, but one has to start somewhere. It is sometimes claimed that one starts with data, from which a model is constructed. But why those data? And how should those data be interpreted? The answers reveal informal models that precede the acquisition of data. (Gunawardena, 2014, p. 3441)

Accordingly, this section will discuss different types of models according to their level of formality. To emphasize how informal models often lead to the creation of formal ones, we will begin with the mental models that precede all other models and move our way up to mathematical models. This sequence is not only about what kind of models typically come first in the investigation of a target phenomenon, but also the types of assumptions they make. As Gunawardena notes, informal models can also be distinguished from formal ones by how explicit their assumptions are. He argues that informal models, unlike formal ones, 'have two classes of assumptions: those that are explicit in the model itself, or foreground assumptions; and those that are only implicit but potentially significant, or background assumptions' (Gunawardena, 2014, p. 3441). As I shall now argue, informal models have their distinct advantages and purposes as compared to formal ones. We will begin with models that rely the most heavily on implicit and background assumptions (i.e. mental models) and work ourselves to models that rely on explicit assumptions only (i.e. mathematical models).

3.1 Mental Models

Although evolutionary biologists often lament the misunderstandings of evolution by members of the public (and even within sciences outside of evolutionary biology), it is clear that almost anyone familiar with evolution now has something like a mental model of the process of evolution (d'Apollonia et al., 2004). This doesn't mean that those models are sophisticated or accurate. The folk understanding of evolution may involve many mistaken ideas and assumptions (see Abenes & Caballes, 2020; De Santis, 2021), such as evolution being goal directed and leading to greater perfection, or the idea that natural selection is an agent selecting the best and discarding the rest. But that doesn't change the fact that evolution is in some way represented in the minds of specialists and non-specialists alike. It is therefore interesting to understand these mental models, since they are ultimately involved in the building of diagrammatic, concrete, or mathematical models of evolution.

Recalling the difference between foreground and background assumptions, it should be clear that mental models rely the most on background assumptions; that is on the implicit knowledge and assumptions of the 'modeller'. If you have ever had someone trying to explain a scientific concept to you, you may have noticed gaps in their explanation coming from implicit knowledge and assumptions on the part of the explainer. Indeed, the main hallmark of a good teacher is the ability to make these implicit assumptions explicit, in order to be understood by students. But this may not be necessary for your own understanding and only becomes required when you are trying to teach others and are trying to examine the assumptions of your own thinking in more detail.

When Darwin endeavoured to understand the origin of species, he did not have a detailed and worked out idea of how long it would take for species to evolve. Parallels with artificial selection gave him a comparison class but his theorizing was largely vague on the question of timescales, tying himself to current estimates in geology regarding the age of the Earth as well as the durations of other time periods. This vagueness afforded him the flexibility to model the gradual process of evolution by natural selection in his mind, but suffered from an inability to make precise predictions about how long it would take. Both due to his lack of mathematical ability and fear of making his theory easily dismissible by including premature calculations about time, the Origin of Species has largely remained free of precise predictions. Indeed, some of the few calculations and speculations Darwin did make about time prompted religious and scientific opponents of his theory to offer damning attacks (Gunawardena, 2014, p. 3442). Similarly, Darwin had little understanding of the mechanisms behind inheritance, treating the similarity between offspring and parent largely as a background assumption in his reasoning. This almost led to the rejection of the theory, if it hadn't been for the merger between

Mendelian genetics and Darwinism that eventually filled this black box in Darwin's theory (Otsuka, 2019). Yet, by leaving these aspects of his theory fairly vague, and including an element of chance, Darwin was able to come up with many ideas and explanations for previously disparate and strange biological phenomena that were later confirmed. Indeed, if Darwin had left inheritance and time out of the informal models he presented in the Origin, he *might* have faced less criticism. However, if Darwin had been forced to explicitly bring out all of his assumptions in the form of even more precise and testable predictions, his theory could easily have been rejected, without allowing for further refinements. Background and implicit assumptions can thus play crucial roles for the creation of entirely new research programmes. As Gunawardena argues:

> Whether a particular fact is in the foreground or relegated to the background depends on the problem at hand and the questions being asked. This allows us to tolerate much ambiguity. Does X mean chicken X or fly X? Does it matter? When it does, background becomes foreground; when it does not, foreground becomes background. The ever-present inconsistencies in biological life can be managed by relegating some findings to a background limbo until they can be reliably brought into the foreground or rejected. Informal models are readily corrected and updated and change organically with the changing context. (Gunawardena, 2014, p. 3442)

The development of novel scientific theories, as exemplified by Darwin's work, hinges on mental modelling. Depending on what aspects of nature one is trying to understand, some assumptions come into the foreground whereas others move into the background. This is a fundamental feature of how our minds cognitively represent things to model the world (Nehm et al., 2009). It is easy to notice that even in one's own theorizing some assumptions are delegated so far to the background that one isn't even consciously aware of them as soon as you are trying to explain your implicit model-based reasoning to others. This is where communication with others is crucial for refining mental models. In order to communicate mental models effectively to others, whether verbally or in writing, many implicit assumptions need to be made explicit and that allows one to recognize and describe them. As we shall see now, this is what Darwin did when he tried to work out the general process of evolution by natural selection in his writing.

3.2 Verbal and Linguistic Models

If there are mental models, then it should be easy to see that models can also be verbal or written. This is not to suggest that words themselves are models in virtue of representing states in the world, but rather that language can be used to create models. Indeed, as Dimech points out: 'Darwin used models in the form of invented, idealized narratives to display how the process of natural selection works' (2017, p. 20). The most prominent case in The Origin of Species is perhaps Darwin's usage of artificial selection as a model for natural selection. His mental model of the similarities between the two types of selection enabled him to offer the following linguistic model:

> I have seen it gravely remarked, that it was most fortunate that the strawberry began to vary just when gardeners began to attend closely to this plant. No doubt the strawberry had always varied since it was cultivated, but the slight varieties had been neglected. As soon, however, as gardeners picked out individual plants with slightly larger, earlier, or better fruit, and raised seedlings from them, and again picked out the best seedlings and bred from them, then, there appeared (aided by some crossing with distinct species) those many admirable varieties of the strawberry which have been raised during the last thirty or forty years. (Darwin, 1859, pp. 41–42)

Here, Darwin makes the case that varieties have always existed within species, but that we typically didn't notice the minor ones. It is only with the advent of agriculture that even the most minor variations became significant to us, triggering artificial selection and yielding marked phenotypic changes within just a few years. With this mental model constructed in the mind of his readers, Darwin moves on to use this model as a surrogate by which to make us consider whether heritable variations in nature could lead to similar accumulations of gradual change, giving rise to natural as opposed to artificial selection:

> No one supposes that all the individuals of the same species are cast in the very same mould. These individual differences are highly important for us, as they afford materials for natural selection to accumulate, in the same manner as man can accumulate in any given direction individual differences in his domesticated productions. (Darwin, 1859, p. 45)

This is more than just the provision of arguments in favour of his view. Darwin deliberately builds an informal model with the ingredients of variation and selection within a population, using artificial selection as a surrogate for natural selection to provide a proof of concept. Even today, numerous evolutionary biology papers include stories of this kind to offer informal models representing target phenomena of interest, before moving on to offer experiments and formal models. As Gunawardena puts it: 'Informal models do not necessarily lead to fast thinking, but they encourage intuitive plausibility over logical deduction' (Gunawardena, 2014, p. 3442).

Even philosophers of biology themselves sometimes admit to the use of such models. Pierrick Bourrat for instance, in his recent Element on the levels of selection, dedicates several pages to the elaboration of a 'simple verbal model to show that the conditions under which fitness [between individuals and the groups constituted by them] could become indefinitely decoupled cannot be met in most situations' (Bourrat, 2021, p. 56). Yet, because of the complexity of evolution, verbal models also allow a lot of room 'for error and oversight in verbal chains of logic' (Servedio et al., 2014, p. 2). While the assumptions are made more explicit in verbal models than in mental models, the models nevertheless still rely on many unspoken background assumptions. In this, they are similar to diagrammatic models, which (while admittedly relying on a different medium) often do not make their background assumptions explicit.

But before we turn to diagrammatic and pictorial models, let me emphasize that the apparent weakness of verbal models can also be a strength. Indeed, they 'often derive their influence by functioning as lightning rods for debate about exactly which biological factors and processes are (or should be) under consideration and how they will interact over time' (Servedio et al., 2014, p. 2). Thus, verbal and written models often function as a tool for social communication and refinement, that can lead background assumptions of mental models to be made explicit and testable in more precise mathematical models.

Unfortunately, philosophers have paid scant attention to the roles of such models. Some philosophers of models, such as (Weisberg, 2013), only allow for verbal descriptions of models, not the existence of verbal models themselves, but this artificial limitation on the typology of models has been questioned (Dimech, 2017; O'Connor & Weatherall, 2016; Veit, 2023). As Darwin's models nicely illustrate, verbal argument is no mere placeholder for the description of some other model, whether mathematical or otherwise. They constitute models in their own right that may or may not also be turned into a different medium, such as a mathematical model. As Dimech puts it, 'what matters for determining whether types of objects are models or not is whether scientists use such objects as idealized intermediaries to study the world' (Dimech, 2017, p. 24). For a longer in-depth discussion of verbal models within Darwin's *On the Origin of Species*, see Dimech's (2017) dedicated article on the topic. Let us now turn to another informal type of models: diagrammatic and pictorial models.

3.3 Diagrammatic and Pictorial Models

Modern evolutionary biology abounds with diagrammatic and pictorial models that fulfil their representational roles through two-dimensional images. This is evident in contemporary doctoral studies in the field, which lead many students to become experts at using modern software to create such models; a stark contrast to earlier evolutionists who could only provide rough and ready drawings by hand unless they had significant artistic talent. It has become increasingly common to offer diagrammatic models in leading journals such as *Nature* and *Science*, reflecting the unique capacity of such models to represent a lot of information in a concise and useful manner.

In Section 2, I mentioned that philosophers of science often use maps, as a paradigmatic case for understanding how models can represent. Evolutionary biologists interested in the distribution and evolution of species naturally also have an interest in maps. In the fields of phylogeography and biogeography, evolutionary biologists often use geographic maps to explain the distribution and ancestry of species (Loughney et al., 2021). This is perhaps most strikingly illustrated by the use of maps showing the drift of continents, to explain species distributions such as the striking prevalence of marsupials in Australia and South America (Cotner & Wassenberg, 2020, pp. 37–38).

However, when it comes to the dense forest of diagrammatic models within evolutionary biology, one tree stands out among rest. While Darwin didn't include any mathematical models in *The Origin of Species*, he included a single diagram that visually represented the tree of life (see Figure 1).

In Figure 1, the labels A to L on the horizontal axis represent different populations, with time being represented on the vertical axis. This illustrates the branching species may undergo over time, aiming to explain the diversity of species we find today. Some of the branches (representing populations) go extinct due to variations in their traits (or chance events such as a forest fire), whereas others are favoured by natural selection and continue. For Darwin, it seems clear that this diagrammatic model was useful to visualize and build a mental model for himself of the origin of species diversity. Indeed, already in 1837 he had sketched his first version of this tree (Darwin, 1837, p. 36).

Today, such figures are ubiquitous in evolutionary biology to help visualize the relationships between species. We call them *phylogenetic trees*. To use a thought experiment, we might imagine early evolutionists

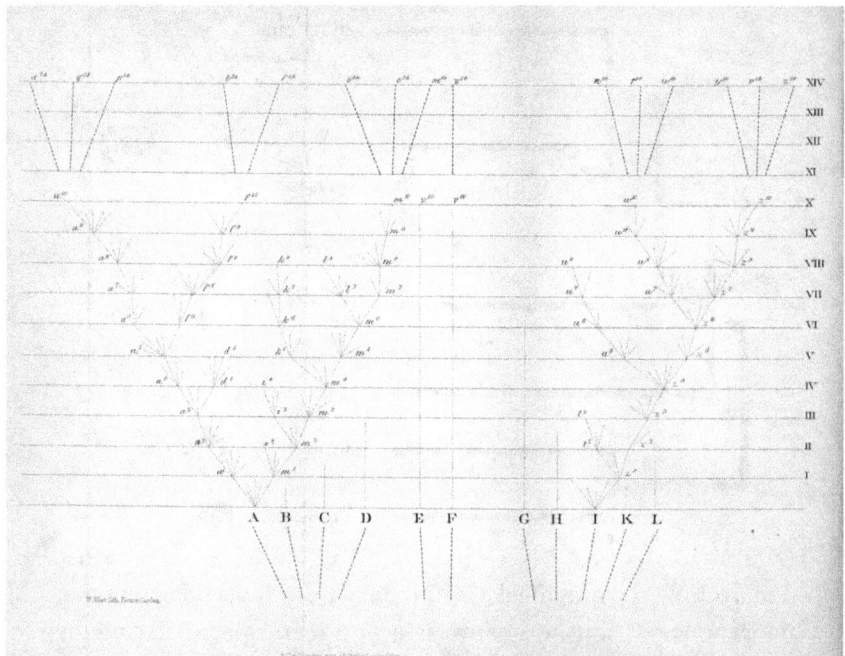

Figure 1 Darwin's Phylogenetic Tree from *On the Origin of Species* (Darwin, 1859, p. 116a(v)). Reproduced by the kind permission of the Syndics of Cambridge University Library.

hypothesizing about the evolutionary relationships between hippopotamuses and elephants, creating phylogenetic trees depicting close relatedness based on their physiological similarities. However, subsequent evidence from genetics, embryology, behaviour, and other areas could quickly undermine such a model and lead to an updated phylogenetic tree, as shown in Figure 2. We will use this example later in Section 4 to illustrate different methods of testing such models, but for now, it is important to emphasize that such models are always partial, only offering a snapshot of the tree of life.

While we could imagine a tree that specifies the histories of all species from the present back through to the origin of life, such a tree would not only be impossible to create (due to gaps in the data), but also useless in the sense of being visually impenetrable except as depicting the tree of life as a whole. Consider, for instance, the immense task of mapping out the millions of contemporary species that would have to be presented at the tips of such a tree. In any such model, there is a choice of how many taxa to include, giving us a trade-off between a simple model depicting only a limited number of taxa, or a more expansive one that is perhaps

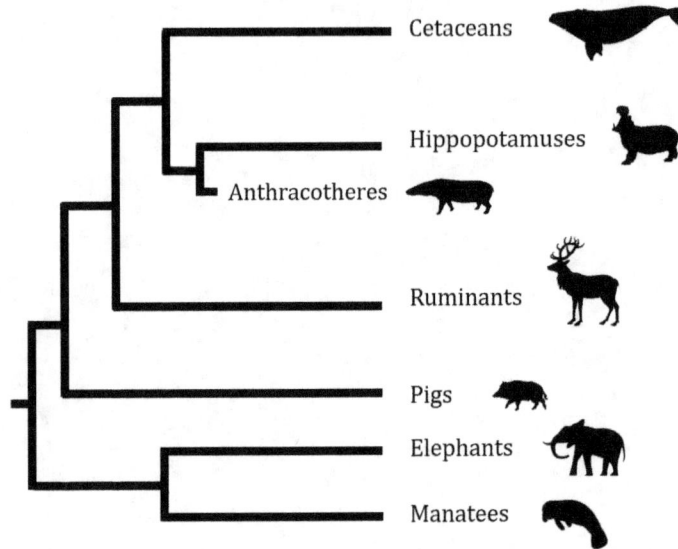

Figure 2 A very simplified evolutionary tree model depicting the phylogenetic relationships between large aquatic mammals and their closest relatives. The anthracotheres family of hippopotamus-like ungulates went extinct, which is why their branch does not reach the present. This diagrammatic model was kindly created by Erola Fenollosa for this Element.

more accurate, but less useful to make a specific argumentative point, which highlights how different goals for models can trade off against each other.

Unfortunately, misconceptions about evolutionary trees are quite common, such as the belief that time represents progress or that some species are more 'evolved' than others. This may in part be due to the way they represent information (Gregory, 2008; Meir et al., 2007). Thus, we should also be careful to also recognize the ways diagrammatic models may hinder science. As Griesemer early on recognized:

> Diagrams can also hinder theory-construction in virtue of their representational power: they can become so entrenched in our way of theorizing that they outlive their theoretical usefulness. In serving to represent causal theories which function heuristically in the background of a given theory of interest, diagrams may provide strong ontological constraints on the way the foreground theory is understood. (Griesemer, 1990, p. 81)

Some researchers have made just this point with the tree of life model, arguing that it fits only poorly with microbiology for example, where speciation does not branch in the same way and gene exchange between lineages is common (O'Malley & Koonin, 2011). This is why it is important to recognize that phylogenetic tree models have a fit for purpose and are designed with specific goals in mind, such as to depict the split between humans and our last common ancestors with the other Great apes. Their usefulness will always be relative to this purpose and should not be applied beyond this context.

Computational advances, however, can partially reduce these limits and the trade-offs between alternative models of the tree of life. The first attempt at this has been *Open Tree of Life* (Hinchliff et al., 2015), with the most sophisticated version found in OneZoom (Rosindell & Harmon, 2012; Sack, 2018; Wong & Rosindell, 2022) allowing it to represent on a single website over 2.2 million species via more than a hundred thousand pictures that one can zoomed in and out from.[1] In this case, is this still a single model or should we speak of a combination of thousands of diagrammatic models?

With mathematical models in evolutionary biology, such as Maynard Smith's Hawk–Dove Game, one could easily be led to believe that it is only a single model. Typically, however, even named models such as *The Hawk–Dove Model* often refer to a broad cluster of models with different parameters and idealizations, rather than one particular model, to show how a result or mechanism can be robust.

Admittedly, this is not what goes on in the OneZoom model of the tree of life. This collection of individual models is not about testing the robustness of a particular hypothesis, but rather about offering a comprehensive and interactive model that can help illustrate the idea that all life has a common origin.

Some computational models, such as those constructed in NetLogo (a programming language for agent-based models), allow one to simulate different evolutionary games, such as the prisoner's dilemma (Wilensky, 2002) while changing parameters in a very easy to understand and accessible manner and accompanying visual models demonstrating changes in a population. This could be similarly seen as offering an interactive model to understand evolutionary dynamics. Playing around with models such as OneZoom and these evolutionary game theoretic models, one cannot help but feel a sense of deeper understanding and appreciation for evolution than with static models, whether in the form of a single diagram or

---

[1] OneZoom is being continuously updated with new features, such as guided tours. To play around with this interactive visual model of the tree of life and enhance your mental model of evolution, please visit: www.onezoom.org.

mathematical model. These models effectively refine our mental models of evolution, by offering visual models that represent more abstract relations or processes, which is precisely why they are useful as teaching tools. Thus, while we can immediately observe striking differences between the goals behind pictorial and computational models and the means through which they are achieved, such as their representational means, we can nevertheless discover important similarities between them, such as representing the same target system.

This also highlights some of the questions we will try to address in Section 4 of this Element: What is the relationship between models of different types? And how can we test models of evolution? But before we turn to these questions, there are still a few types of models that have yet to be discussed.

3.4 Concrete Models

While mental, verbal, diagrammatic, and mathematical models are all fairly abstract, this group of models are concrete. Following Weisberg, we can define such concrete models as 'real, physical objects that are intended to stand in representational relationship to some real or imagined system, set of systems, or generalized phenomenon' (Weisberg, 2013, p. 24). Can we build tangible models of evolution? Concrete models typically rely on real-world equivalents of a target-system, such as a miniaturized version of the San Francisco Bay, with real water. Surely, many will say that this is not possible for evolutionary models. Creationist critics of evolution often accuse that no one has seen evolution with their own eyes. Yet... Could we imagine a special creator that plays around with the evolutionary process? In their textbook on evolution, Bergstrom and Dugatkin ask students to imagine an evolutionary biologist with special powers:

- Watch as tens of thousands of generations of evolution take place before your eyes.
- Manipulate the physical environment to control nutrient availability, temperature, spatial structure, and other features, and manipulate the biotic environment, adding or removing competitors, predators, and parasites.
- Create multiple parallel universes with the same starting conditions in which to watch evolution unfold in replicate worlds.
- Move organisms around in a 'time machine' so that they can interact with – and compete against – their ancestors or their descendants.
- Go back in time to rerun evolution from any point, under the same or different environmental conditions.
- Easily measure both allele frequencies and fitnesses to accuracies of 0.1% or smaller. (Bergstrom & Dugatkin, 2012, pp. 78–79)

This may seem like a dream outside of computer simulations, but this is in fact what is frequently done in the field of experimental evolution. As they point out, no better example of this has been provided than the Long-Term Evolution Experiment (LTEE) by Richard Lenski and his collaborators, who have created such a model system with *Escherichia coli* bacteria. As of their recent announcement on their dedicated LTEE website, they have now passed the incredible number of 80,000 generations.[2] The LTEE thus 'encompasses more generations than there have been in the entire history of our species, *Homo sapiens*' (Bergstrom & Dugatkin, 2012, p. 79). While it would take many lifetimes to observe evolutionary change in a species like ours, microbial populations in a lab may undergo evolutionary change in mere days, allowing evolution to be observed, simulated, and intervened on right in front of our eyes. *E. coli*, for instance, can reproduce around once every 20 minutes under ideal conditions. Populations can be frozen at any stage during this process to allow a replaying of the evolutionary tape (Gould, 1990), such that we can observe whether evolution will lead to the same or different outcomes from the same starting positions. The LTEE has shown, for instance, that genetic drift plays a major role in shaping populations, where future generations are strongly influenced by chance and not just past beneficial adaptations (Plutynski, 2001). Such physical simulations of evolution do not require the use of mathematical models, but can operate directly on biological populations.

Nevertheless, we should be careful to uphold the distinction between models, simulations, and experiments at least somewhat. Not every experimental population undergoing evolution is necessarily a model; otherwise, we might as well call all experiments models. This would render the distinction between modeller and experimentalist obsolete. However, sometimes experimental populations do indeed constitute models, when they are intended to represent another target rather than examined for their own sake. Biologists sometimes employ model organisms that are intended as surrogate systems for other targets, such as the use of chimpanzees or mice in human medical research (Ankeny & Leonelli, 2020). But these are not evolutionary models. Evolution is not about individuals, but about populations. Thus, we can analogously use the term model populations to better describe experimental populations used to understand evolutionary processes in another specific target or more generally evolutionary processes as such wherever they may occur.

---

[2] https://the-ltee.org/80000-generations-new-olympic-record/

Thanks to several efforts by philosophers of biology, the importance of such concrete models was recognized early on within the philosophy of biology (Griesemer, 1990; Plutynski, 2001). But concrete models also have a special role within the philosophy of models because of their unique position as models operating in the same ontological realm as their target systems. [For the non-philosophers reading this Element, ontology is the metaphysical study of which category of the world things belong to. In the case of a concrete model and its target system, it is the real world for both.] Indeed, whereas all other models (especially mathematical) are often viewed with a more critical stance by philosophers of science, concrete models seem to get a pass. Frigg even calls all other models '*non-material models*', which can include both formal and informal models (Frigg, 2022, p. 248). This gives us another way of categorizing different types of models. But should such models be exempt from ontological criticisms?

Frigg goes so far as to state that 'these models are commonplace material objects and as such similarity is no problem for them' from the perspective of ontology. Even if the similarity problem does exist for concrete models 'they do not give rise to ontological questions over and above the questions that one can ask about every other material object' (Frigg, 2022, p. 248). Griesemer similarly states that material models 'are robust to some changes of theoretical perspective because they are literally embodiments of phenomena' (Griesemer, 1990, p. 80). This is because other models are assumed to necessarily have higher degrees of abstraction and idealization, due to their different mediums. Even biologists using model populations express the idea that 'only studies on natural populations can address the issue of whether populations in the real world tend to show stable dynamic behavior' (Mueller & Joshi, 2000, p. 5). But model populations in evolutionary biology are still highly idealized models when they are used to model general evolutionary dynamics or dynamics within other species, making this difference one of degree and not of kind.

For instance, Paul Rainey and his collaborators have spent a lot of time studying the potential emergence of multicellular individuality in the lab, using the bacterium *Pseudomonas fluorescens* (Hammerschmidt et al., 2014). The goal of this work was not to argue that *P. fluorescens* was at the origin of multicellularity individuality. This transition happened several times in evolutionary history, but rather to investigate plausible evolutionary scenarios and dynamics for how it might happen (Black et al., 2020; Hammerschmidt et al., 2014; Rose et al., 2020). This approach was explicitly interventionist, with the goal of biasing selection towards mutations that may be conducive towards multicellular group formation, reproduction, and cohesion. This reflects the observation by Keller that there are 'models for' intervention rather than just 'models of' the target (Keller, 2000).

It is hardly surprising, then, that the work of Rainey and his collaborators has received a lot attention by philosophers (Neto et al., 2023; Veit, 2019b, 2022), including collaborative work that offers models for how this transition from single cells to genuine higher-level individuals may have happened (Bourrat et al., 2024). The goal of such research is not necessarily to explain how things *actually* happened, but to offer a plausible explanation for how something may *possibly* have happened. Philosophers of science have introduced the distinction between how-actually and how-possibly explanations to emphasize that explanations can usefully focus on plausible scenarios, without those necessarily having occurred in the real world (Bokulich, 2014; Resnik, 1991). Indeed, due to the sparsity of historical data, this is often what evolutionary biologists aim for instead. As Plutynski points out, such model populations are not necessarily meant 'to *prove* the relative significance of one or another factor in the evolutionary process, but to provide a plausibility argument' (Plutynski, 2001, p. 233). This will be of relevance in Section 4, when we discuss the ways in which models of evolution can be tested.

In conclusion, model populations play incredibly important roles within evolutionary biology. Indeed, they blur the supposed hard distinction between models and experiments that is commonly made. The interaction between these models and mathematical models is of central importance in much of evolutionary biology, but has not yet been given sufficient attention by philosophers of biology, and I expect this literature to grow significantly in the future. For further reading, I recommend the book *Stability in Model Populations* by Mueller & Joshi (2000), who offer a detailed analysis of laboratory studies on model populations (with a special focus on flies such as *Drosophila*), as well as Plutynski's (2001) analysis of Lenski's LTEE and similar model populations of *Drosophila*.

Let us now turn to the final type of models I discuss in this Element: mathematical models.

3.5 Mathematical Models

We have moved our way from the most informal to the most formal types of models. Philosophers of biology, as well as philosophers of models, have spent most of their time thinking about mathematical models. This applies even to this Elements series, with Otsuka's (2019) Element on the role of mathematics in evolutionary biology and Odenbaugh's (2019) Element on ecological models, both of which focus on mathematical models and which I recommend as further readings for this section. But it is precisely because of a comparative neglect of non-mathematical models that I wanted to first give the others some attention. While I haven't dedicated the whole Element to mathematical models, they nevertheless now play an irreplaceable role within modern evolutionary biology. This is a significant change from Darwin's time. While Darwin provided verbal models of evolution by natural selection, it is often said that it was only with the advancement of mathematical models that the theory became precise, leading to the development of a mature science of evolutionary biology (Bergstrom & Dugatkin, 2012; Otsuka, 2019). In the transition to mathematical models, assumptions implicit in verbal and mental models come to be specified, to allow for collective usage. Indeed, as Gunawardena argues, in 'marked contrast to their informal counterparts, they cannot tolerate any form of ambiguity: all assumptions are in the foreground, and there is no background. If it is not in the equations, it is not in the model' (Gunawardena, 2014, p. 3442).

Philosophers of science readily acknowledge that mathematical models are now the primary tool in evolutionary theory. Lloyd, for instance, argues that the 'main reason that models should be considered in any description of the structure of evolutionary theory is that models themselves are the primary theoretical tools used by evolutionary biologists' (Lloyd, 1994, p. 9). It is simply not possible to create concrete models for the many purposes for which mathematical models are designed and used. Biological reality is many ways less flexible than mathematically constructed systems. As Plutynski notes, 'mathematical models can answer questions that laboratory models cannot' (Plutynski, 2001, p. 233). For instance, microbial or insect populations may simply not be similar enough to bird populations to allow them to stand in a useful model–target relationship for some questions. Here, a mathematical model may feature many more of the relevant similarities, despite the target and model being different kinds of objects altogether. In their textbook on evolution, Bergstrom and Dugatkin praise college education in economics and physics for preparing students to translate real-world questions into mathematics and figuring out how to solve them, and take this as something to be emulated by evolutionary biologists (Bergstrom & Dugatkin, 2012, p. xxii). We can thus firmly assert that mathematical models play irreplaceable roles within evolutionary biology and are therefore worth philosophical analysis.

To do their work, formal models typically rely on equations and mathematical symbols. This mathematical structure is generally meant to stand in a similarity relationship with a real-world target. Recall the Hawk–Dove Model discussed in Section 2. Here we had the mathematical symbols V and C representing the fitness value of a resource in nature and the cost of a resource conflict in a particular population. The payoff matrix shown in Table 1 gave us the payoff values for different interactions in the game, intended to represent real conflict situations as they may occur in nature, but idealized so as to exclude other irrelevant factors. The expected payoff of each strategy depends on the probability of encountering hawks or doves.

We can now break down this model mathematically. Let p be the proportion of hawks in the population and $1-p$ be the proportion of doves.

Expected Fitness for hawk: (U_H)
Conditional fitness of a hawk facing another hawk: $\frac{V-C}{2}$ (probability p)
Conditional fitness of a hawk facing a dove: V (probability $1-p$)

$$U_H = p \cdot (V-C)/2 + (1-p) \cdot V$$

$$U_H = p\frac{V-C}{2} + V - pV$$

$$U_H = V - pV + p\frac{V-C}{2}$$

Expected Fitness for dove: (U_D)
Conditional fitness of a dove facing a hawk: 0 (probability p)
Conditional fitness of a dove facing another dove: $\frac{V}{2}$ (probability $1-p$)

$$U_D = p \cdot 0 + (1-p) \cdot V/2$$

$$U_D = (1-p)V/2$$

Both strategies should be equal in fitness in an equilibrium:

$$U_H = U_D$$

$$V - pV + p\frac{V-C}{2} = (1-p)\frac{V}{2}$$

Solve for p:

$$V - pV + \frac{p(V-C)}{2} = \frac{V}{2} - \frac{pV}{2}$$

$$\frac{V}{2} = pV - \frac{pV}{2} - \frac{pV}{2} + \frac{pC}{2}$$

$$\frac{V}{2} = \frac{pC}{2}$$

$$p = \frac{V}{C}$$

This shows that if the payoff V is higher than the cost C, hawks will dominate, whereas the reverse situation will result in a mixed strategy. If $V = 1$ and $C = 2$, there will be an even split of hawks and doves. While the Hawk Dove Game is highly idealized and only consists of simple equations, it nevertheless provides a sense of explanation: a how-possibly explanation (Resnik, 1991) that can in principle explain potential cases of conflicts over resources (or, for that matter, the relative absence of them), even if the actual explanation for real cases might differ. Indeed, as Gunawardena points out, mathematical models are not typically used to 'test' assumptions, but rather to aid us in precise and rigorous reasoning:

> Formal models are extremely brittle, and the tiniest change in assumptions requires new conclusions to be derived, which may differ from the previous conclusions. The value of a formal model does not rest on its ability to deal with assumptions, in which it compares very poorly to an informal model, but on its capacity for reasoning by logical deduction. (Gunawardena, 2014, p. 3442)

This is one of the reasons why Maynard Smith (1982) dedicates a large proportion of his book to discussing more complex versions of basic games such as the Hawk–Dove Game. The initial model offers a so-called proof-of-concept, a mathematical proof for an initially verbal argument about the dynamics of resource conflicts. This is far from trivial. As Servedio et al. point out, when 'hidden assumptions are altered or removed, the predicted outcomes and resulting inferences of the formal model may differ from, or even contradict, those of the verbal model' (Servedio et al., 2014, p. 3). Many attempts to strengthen a verbal argument through a mathematical model will result in undermining the original argument, either by highlighting mistaken assumptions or by revealing a failure in the logic of the argument. But one of their most useful roles is to make explicit the hidden assumptions that may differ between scientists disagreeing on an issue. Such proof-of-concept models are incredibly common in evolutionary biology and often do have little connection to data, when long timescales are concerned (see discussion in Servedio et al., 2014).

Nevertheless, by exploring a variety of more complex versions of the same basic game, we can learn how different conditions may change basic dynamics within evolutionary game theory, as well as which dynamics are robust against different kinds of perturbations, thereby moving us beyond a mere proof-of-concept. One of the most obvious changes that can be made to such a model is the inclusion of genetic details or combination with population genetics models (McGlothlin et al., 2022), though such models inevitably become more complex without the simple '*like begets like*' assumption that parents will give rise to identical offspring. As we shall discuss in the next section, this kind of *robustness analysis*, which changes aspects of a model to examine whether and how they change the result, is fundamental to 'tests' of mathematical models of evolution. They help us to reason through different biological scenarios without the need to design new experiments altogether.

Let me now turn to statistical models and computer simulations. Earlier in this Element, I identified them as instances of formal models, but we may wonder whether they constitute different categories from mathematical models or should be considered as instances of them. I will first consider the former option.

Statistical models are clearly mathematical in nature. Nevertheless, they also function quite differently from the typical mathematical model scientists might build to understand a system. As Sober notes, unlike statistical models, mathematical models are usually understood by scientists to refer to 'a simplified hypothesis; it purports to explain or predict a set of observations without trying to represent all the factors that are relevant' (Sober, 2008, p. 80). Statistical models are instead largely used to analyse large amounts of data and make inferences from them. This can then allow us to find important relationships between variables, for instance through a regression model. Frigg describes statistical models as 'a mathematical representation of the observed data' from scientific observations (Frigg, 2022, p. 473). This needs to be distinguished from the more general modelling of the influence of chance in evolutionary processes, where evolutionary biologists ubiquitously draw on many statistical methods, such as Bayesian methods and maximum likelihood methods (Romeijn, 2022). Indeed, it is worth emphasizing that evolutionary biologists have innovated many statistical methods to deal with their unique scientific problems, especially in population genetics models (Bergstrom & Dugatkin, 2012).

While statistical models do typically have different goals from mathematical models, they often operate in tandem with them, such as when data is used to test predictions of mathematical models of a target system. However, they are still worth distinguishing in a philosophical analysis of models. Statistical data models of the genetic code of different species are, after all, often at the foundation for the construction of phylogenetic trees, as discussed above, to represent such data visually. Indeed, they are both data models, though in one case represented mathematically and in the other visually.

Just as with other models, statistical models still rely on idealizations, such as the assumption that relationships between variables will be linear or that there are no variables other than those. While statistical models are typically closer to reality due to their use of real-world data, they can in some cases be more idealized than mathematical models. Furthermore, the line between these types of models can be further blurred when theoretical models are filled in with data in order to test them, as we shall discuss in Section 4. Moreover, mathematical models are not constructed in a vacuum, but are often implicitly guided by the experience modellers have gained from dealing with various biological data sets such as in statistical models. Nevertheless, compared to some other fields of biology that do not have to deal with the distant past, such as biomedical research, evolutionary biology makes understandably less use of statistical models due to a sparsity of data. But statistical methods themselves could not be removed from evolutionary biology without collapsing the entire field, emphasizing their importance and showing that there is no way of drawing a sharp boundary between mathematical and statistical models within the field. Statistical models are therefore best analysed as a special subtype of mathematical models, rather than a separate category.

Finally, we can look at computational models. Weisberg (2013) distinguishes between mathematical models and computational models. Whereas mathematical models can be seen as consisting of equations that can be solved analytically, computational models are meant to simulate change across time through stepwise processes or computer algorithms. However, O'Connor and Weatherall (2016) argue that the replicator dynamics, which is a tool in evolutionary game theory for modelling the change of frequency of strategies across time, can be described both as a discrete trajectory or as a smooth trajectory than can easily be transformed from one to the other, with modellers using them interchangeably (pp. 620–621).[3] Is there a crucial difference here between the mathematical and computational version of the model? Consider the following continuous-time equation from Weibull's textbook in evolutionary game theory (Weibull, 1995, p. 72):

$$\frac{dx_i}{dt} = \left[u(i,x) - u(x,x)\right] \cdot x_i$$

---

[3] Evolutionary game theory models have also been used to model cultural evolution, for example, moral norms in human societies (Veit, 2019a), but within the confines of this Element, I will restrict myself to biological evolution.

Here, $\frac{dx_i}{dt}$ stands for the rate of change of x_i over time, which in turn stands for the proportion of individuals within a population playing the strategy i. The payoff of an individual playing i is represented by $u(i,x)$ whereas $u(x,x)$ stands for the average population fitness. If the difference is positive, i does better than the population average and will thus increase in frequency. This in turn is impacted by how many individuals already play the strategy, with the reverse happening when the difference is negative. This formulation can easily be turned into the following discrete-time equation:

$$x_i(t+1) = x_i(t) + \Delta x_i$$

Here, $x_i(t)$ stands for the proportion of individuals playing i at time t. Δx_i represents the change in frequencies of strategies across one discrete step in time. As O'Connor and Weatherall (2016) argue, nothing in a choice like this rests on a difference in actual representational content, instead of ease of analysis, with the distinctions between mathematical and computational models actually obscuring 'the most important aspects about how the models are used' (p. 621).

This is a stronger argument than the more common one that computational models simply constitute a special case of mathematical models. Consider, for instance, Giere's reductive explanation of computer simulations as just a special instance of mathematical modelling:

> A computer simulation is just a fancy way of investigating the mathematical features of an abstract model characterized by a set of equations. The physical computer puts constraints on what sorts of functions can be used in the characterization of the model and how fast they can be solved. But this is no different in principle from the limitations of a person solving differential equations by hand. The main limitation to computer simulation is that literally everything has to be characterized symbolically. If one wants to model an organism in an environment, one has to model the environment as well. On the other hand, computer simulations have the desirable feature that everything about the model is explicitly represented. (Giere, 2001, p. 1060)

Agreeing with Giere, Frigg maintains that 'computational models are also mathematical models and the class of formal models in fact coincides with the class of mathematical models' (Frigg, 2022, p. 248). This is the view I adopt within the context of this Element. While different applications of formal models may require different approaches, that does not itself justify the claim that there is some deeper categorical difference here. Weisberg himself considers this option, admitting that 'computational operations are at base mathematical operations' and 'are formally described in terms of states and transitions' that are explained within the context of 'discrete mathematics' (Weisberg, 2013, p. 19). However, he maintains that we should make an epistemological distinction, that is, in terms of how they generate knowledge. Whereas the *explanans* in one case is an algorithm, in the other it is the mathematical structure (Weisberg, 2013, p. 20). But as O'Connor and Weatherall (2016) show, it is easy to turn one into the other, thus making it questionable how much explanatory weight really hangs on the way the model is specified. In the spirit of the model anarchism we examined earlier, we should be careful not to confuse useful *distinctions for* some purpose or other in a specific context where they may be useful, with the establishment of genuine categorical differences that apply across different contexts. In practice, mathematical models can often be solved with parameters treated as symbols, whereas computational models need to give these symbols numerical values. It thus seems best to also treat computational models as a subcategory of mathematical models.

3.6 Summary

In this section, I distinguished between five types of models: mental models, verbal and linguistic models, diagrammatic and pictorial models, concrete models, and mathematical models. However, I have no doubt that some will prefer a different typology of models. One could, for instance, follow Weisberg's distinction between mathematical, computational, and concrete models (Weisberg, 2013), though I have offered some criticism of it here. My goal was neither to offer an exhaustive typology nor to claim that there are some ultimate distinctions to be made within the many things called 'models'. For the purposes of this Element, I simply found the categories presented here to be the most useful way of discussing the diversity of models within evolutionary biology. They serve both as a useful introduction to the philosophy of models for biologists interested in methodology and an illustration of the richness of models within evolutionary biology to philosophers of science. While I haven't discussed models in cultural evolution here, it is worth mentioning that the difficulty of modelling cultural evolution has given rise to fruitful collaborations between philosophers and modellers. The typology offered here may prove useful for this context, though I suspect that cultural evolution comes with its own challenges. For an overview, consider the Element by Lewens (2024) on cultural selection.

I must also emphasize that this typology is not hierarchical. Different goals and contexts may require different models with level of formality being one continuum along which different goals, benefits, and downsides can be identified. Yet, even restricted to the context of evolutionary biology, it appears that such answers would have to be context-specific to the goals of the model. But some typologies are even more simplistic than this, giving a universal ranking of different types of models. As Downes observes, the categorization in Futuyma's (2006) evolutionary biology textbook into 'verbal models, physical models, graphical models, mathematical models, and computer models' is just one instance of the common idea that 'alternate models that can be improved upon by being presented mathematically' (Downes, 2020, pp. 35–36). While I presented mathematical models last, I hope to have made clear that they are by no means inherently superior to other kinds of models. Their increased usage within evolutionary biology is due to improvements in mathematical skill among evolutionary biologists, not because mathematical models are the final endpoint of scientific modelling activity. Different models serve different goals and are complementary to other kinds of goals. While it is true that a mature science will be full of mathematical models to deal with a wealth of data and the complexity of the world, this by no means implies that informal models have lost their purpose(s). Indeed, as we shall see in the next section, different types of models play crucial roles within the context of testing hypotheses.

4 Testing Models of Evolution

For people learning about evolutionary biology, it may come as a surprise that the field is filled with models that make testable predictions. The view of evolution as an untestable theory comes largely from the mistaken assertions by creationist critics, but also from the sheer timescale of evolution, stretching all the way from the origin of life on the Earth, estimated by some to be roughly 4.2 billion years ago (Moody et al., 2024). Furthermore, unlike the largely deterministic nature of sciences such as physics and chemistry, biology is filled with historical 'accidents' that have led to the species that now exist around us. If we were to 'replay' the evolutionary tape of life, starting over again from the same beginnings but with slight changes to conditions along the way, things could look incredibly different. Because of these long evolutionary timescales and the important role of random historical chance, it might be easy to think that it is impossible to test models of evolution. However, this would be a grave mistake. Models of evolution are indeed testable; as we have already seen in the case of the concrete model bacterial populations discussed in the previous section, and as we will go on to discuss in this section.

While philosophers of science, such as Karl Popper, once had dismissive attitudes towards evolutionary biology, deeming it unfalsifiable (Popper, 1957), these attitudes quickly shifted when philosophers started paying real attention to evolutionary theory, and biology at large. Even Popper admitted to his mistake, praising Darwin's achievement: 'The place of an argument that really had no status whatever in science has been taken by an immense number of the most impressive and well tested scientific results' (Popper, 1978, p. 341).[4] Coming from the influence of Popper and others, the ability to make testable predictions is often seen as a necessary component of a genuine science. Evolutionary biologists readily accept this. In their textbook on evolution, Bergstrom and Dugatkin emphasize that the 'scientific process is all about postulating a series of testable hypotheses, ruling out alternatives, and honing in on the hypotheses that seem to best represent what is happening in nature (Mayr, 1982, 1983)' (Bergstrom & Dugatkin, 2012, p. 14). They also list many sources of data that can be used to test evolution, such as molecular genetic data, the fossil record, anatomical morphological data, behavioural data, and data from embryology (Bergstrom & Dugatkin, 2012, p. 5), illustrating the diversity of evidential sources biologists may draw on.

Alternative models can be evaluated against each other by how well they fit the available data coming from any of these sources of evidence. In fact, this already gives us two ways for testing models of evolution that are both widely recognized in the literature: (i) we can test the fit between a model and evidence from one specific field and (ii) we can check how well a model fits the available evidence from a variety of sources. It is possible, for instance, for a model's precise predictions to have a better fit with new data from one area, while fitting worse with the empirical data we have from other fields. Thus, it is important to consider the fit of the model with all the available evidence, rather than just a specific domain. As Odenbaugh emphasizes, a 'model that fits a greater number of data types is more confirmed than one that fits fewer *ceteris paribus*' (Odenbaugh, 2019, p. 22). The question of data-fit is sometimes further broken down into tests of the independent assumptions of a model versus their precise predictions, giving us three means to test models (Lloyd, 1994; Odenbaugh, 2019). But since there is no sharp boundary between testing assumptions and predictions, and assumptions made by models are routinely challenged by competing modellers in just the same way

---

[4] For a more in-depth discussion of Popper's views on evolution, see (Elgin & Sober, 2017; Sonleitner, 1986; Stamos, 1996).

predictions would be, I will largely treat them here as a single type of test. However, I will begin by offering a further justification for this grouping by highlighting what distinguishes modelling in evolutionary biology from other fields.

4.1 Disciplinary Norms and Modelling Practices

Often, the philosophy of models literature is prone to overgeneralizations: a model is analysed in one field, giving rise to generalizations about models as a whole (including in other scientific disciplines). But, as I argued earlier, such extrapolation should be done with more caution. As Parker makes clear, evaluation of models must always be sensitive to the purpose of the models at hand (Parker, 2020). Scientific disciplines (and even sub-fields) can differ greatly in their disciplinary norms and modelling practices, especially regarding the proper goals of models.

This can be illustrated with an easy example. Fields like economics are full of modellers who state that they are only interested in the predictive accuracy of their models, not whether their assumptions are true. This is not true of evolutionary biology, where assumptions are commonly defended as being close enough to reality so as to not undermine the model. As systems biologist Gunawardena emphasizes, formal models 'are only as good as their assumptions; if you make the wrong assumptions, correct mathematics can still produce wrong science; it is more important to understand the assumptions than to believe the conclusions' (Gunawardena, 2014, p. 3444). For instance, Maynard Smith writes in his 1982 book on evolutionary game theory that the 'basic assump-tion of evolutionary game theory – that like begets like – corre-sponds to what we actually know about heredity in most cases' (Maynard Smith, 1982). Detailed information about genetic inheritance can be idealized away to assume that parents will simply transfer all of their traits to their offspring (in the asexual populations typically represented in evolutionary game theory models) because it is realistic enough even when applied to sexual populations at long time horizons. This assumption, however, has not gone without criticism and evolutionary biologists have recently proposed ways to integrate evolutionary game theory models and quantitative genetic models (McGlothlin et al., 2022), reflecting that biologist do care significantly about the accuracy of their assumptions.

By contrast, compare economists such as Milton Friedman, who won the Nobel Memorial Prize in Economic Sciences, and was described by the Economist as the 'most influential economist of the second half of the twentieth century (Keynes died in 1946), possibly of all of it' (The Economist, 2006). His work turned many economists into militant instrumentalists:

> The difficulty in the social sciences of getting new evidence for this class of phenomena and of judging its conformity with the implications of the hypothesis makes it tempting to suppose that other, more readily available, evidence is equally relevant to the validity of the hypothesis-to suppose that hypotheses have not only 'implications' but also 'assumptions' and that the conformity of these 'assumptions' to 'reality' is a test of the validity of the hypothesis *different from* or *additional to* the test by implications. This widely held view is fundamentally wrong and productive of much mischief. (Friedman, 1953, p. 14)

This methodological approach could not be more different from the approach described by Gunawardena: one emphasizes the correctness of assumptions, the other the success of predictions.

Expectedly, Friedman has received a lot of criticism for his radical stance. Rosenberg even argued that his naive instrumentalism 'single-handedly justified' the need for a distinct academic field of philosophy of economics (Rosenberg, 2009, p. 57). Gunawardena has similarly harsh words about the modelling approach of economics:

> It seems unlikely that biology will go the way of economics. In biology, formal models rely on informal models to bridge the gap between reductionism and reality, between what we can logically infer about molecules and what we can discover about life by observation and experiment. We may need to be rigorous, but we had better be right. We need informal models to keep our formal models on the straight and narrow. Our tails need their dogs. Let us spare a thought in passing for our poor colleagues toiling in the 'dismal science' of economics, which seems, from a safe academic distance, to be all tail and no dog. (Gunawardena, 2014, p. 3444)

Informal models play a much larger role in biology than they do in economics, but is that necessarily a flaw in economic science? Despite these criticisms, and advances in empirical economic methods (such as behavioural economics and econometrics), the norms in economic modelling have remained influenced by Friedman's approach that exclusively cares about predictive power.

What to make of this? Must economists learn from evolutionary biologists? Perhaps so, but we should at least allow for the possibility that distinct disciplinary norms may reflect genuine epistemic differences between models and modelling in different sciences. As Brown and

Thomson opened with in their article on the evaluation of models within evolutionary biology: 'Modeling is an exercise in explanation' (Brown & Thomson, 2018, p. 96). The predictions made by models within evolutionary biology typically serve primarily to arrive at better explanations and improve our models, rather than to inform real-world action. This is why this Element is restricted to models in evolutionary biology. While some of the conclusions may extend to other subfields of biology and perhaps even different sciences, I do not treat this as a given, nor do we have the space here to engage with this question in more detail. Thus, whereas economists make a strict distinction between the testing of assumptions and making predictions, I do not see this difference reflected in the practice of evolutionary biologists, where models are in the business of prediction as well as explanation. The assumptions and predictions of models equally stand against the tribunal of evidential support.

This is especially relevant when we consider the different types of models already discussed. In the previous section, we saw that models lend themselves to the formation of new hypotheses. Admittedly, some of the models we've discussed so far are not designed to make predictions. Mental and linguistic models, for example, are often not precise enough to be tested in a satisfactory manner, but they can inspire more formal models for that purpose. Some evolutionary game theory models are general proof-of-principle models without any particular target in mind. Others use these basic games and apply them to explain the phenotypes of actual species, offering a pathway for tests. As Maynard Smith put it, 'there is a contrast between simple models, which are not testable but which may be of heuristic value, and applications of those models to the real world, when testability is an essential requirement' (Maynard Smith, 1982, p. 9). Again, even with the same type of models, we can see that their design will differ drastically depending on the goals we have for them.

Phylogenetic tree models, by contrast, may be better understood as summaries of existing data, which are to be updated if new evidence undermines our current best hypotheses regarding the relationships of descent between different species. For instance, it used to be common to think that hippopotamuses, elephants, and rhinoceroses constituted a joint clade called *Pachydermata* (meaning thick-skinned). We now know that they are not a monophyletic group, relegating the Pachydermata classification to a relic of the past (Bergstrom & Dugatkin, 2012, p. 111). This came from genetic research that revealed hippopotamuses to be the closest relative of cetaceans, such as whales and dolphins (Gatesy et al., 1996; Nikaido et al., 1999). As Figure 2 illustrates, their last common ancestors with elephants lies much deeper in the animal branch of the tree of life. Similarly, it may be surprising to many that manatees share a closer common ancestor with elephants than with cetaceans.

While some models, such as these phylogenetic trees, are effectively data models, we can nevertheless treat them as explanatory and predictive in nature, because their assumptions, as well as their representations of the relations between taxa, remain continually subject to empirical revision. Constructing a particular branching between different species is equivalent to a hypothesis or at least assumption of a model that can be tested. While the public may often think of phylogenetic trees as a largely settled matter, Gregory points out that such models remain the subject of current research:

> [I]t is impossible to know with certainty that any given phylogeny is historically accurate. As a result, any reconstructed phylogenetic tree is a hypothesis about relationships and patterns of branching and thus is subject to further testing and revision with the analysis of additional data. Fully resolved and uncontroversial phylogenies are rare, and as such, the generation, testing, and updating of phylogenetic hypotheses remain an active and sometimes hotly debated area of research. (Gregory, 2008, p. 123)

Due to gaps in the historical record, it is not uncommon for certain branchings in phylogenetic trees to be conjectural and open to future revisions. The assumptions of biological models are thus just as open to tests as their predictions. While models may not be deliberately designed to make predictions, they can nevertheless generate hypotheses or reflect evidence-based estimates that make them testable.

But the role of models is by no means restricted to the generation of new hypotheses. Indeed, the interplay of models with empirical work is quite a bit more complex within evolutionary biology than the common contrasts made by theoreticians and experimentalists may make it seem. As we shall see shortly, it is a mistake to think that the former researchers are in the business of generating hypotheses, whereas the latter are committed to testing them. I will argue that models themselves can be used to test the predictions of other models, while experimental work can lead to new predictions. For simplicity, however, let us begin by surveying how empirical work can test models of evolution.

4.2 Empirical Tests of Evolution

The simplest way models are typically tested is to look at their predictions, using empirical results to examine whether the predictions are correct. However, for the complex systems studied by evolutionary biologists it is often far from straightforward to derive predictions that can prove a model to be 'correct' or 'incorrect'. As mentioned above, models in evolutionary biology are simultaneously examined for both their assumptions and their predictions. One might thus conclude that the most straightforward way of empirically testing a range of alternative models in evolutionary biology is to assess how accurately they describe their target system. Models will be silent on many aspects of the real world, but the relevant features they include should map onto the features of the real-world target they are employed to understand. This may also be described as model fit, although we have to be careful to distinguish fit to a target system from fit to data (Downes, 2020, p. 73). Target systems, such as SARS-CoV-2, may provide us with data that our models can be fitted towards. This provides us with data fit, but not necessarily fit with the target system. After all, data gathering may have been inconclusive, partial, or simply faulty. Thus, comparing data with the predictions and assumptions of our models is far from a neutral enterprise. The data itself has to be assessed in terms of how relevant it is to our models.

Perhaps due to the sparsity of data that Darwin and his contemporaries had available to them, evolutionary biology has become quite adept at uncovering plenty of resources for generating data to validate their models. However, there is one source of evidence that largely trumps all others, viz genetics. It was long hypothesized that chimpanzees (*Pan troglodytes*) were our closest living relatives, but research in comparative genetics has suggested bonobos (*Pan paniscus*) as a possible contender for this spot, thus updating their position in the tree of life to sit equally as close to humans (Gibbons, 2012; Mitchell & Gonder, 2013; Prüfer et al., 2012). Molecular genetics effectively invalidated the assumption made in many phylogenetic tree models that bonobos were more distantly related to us than chimpanzees. The primatologist Frans de Waal aptly commented that the '[t]he story that the bonobo can be safely ignored or marginalized from debates about human origins is now off the table' (quoted in Gibbons, 2012). The revolution in molecular genetics has been perhaps the most significant change in evolutionary biology, allowing challenges to many phylogenetic tree models that were built based on data from the fossil record, behavioural and morphological similarities, and ecological data on the regional habitats of species, among other forms of evidence. No matter how strong the combined evidence from these sources may have been, molecular genetics had the power to undermine even the most well-supported evolutionary hypotheses and assumptions due to its reliability of preserving evolutionary history in the genetic code.

For instance, returning to the previous example, it was found that cetaceans and hippos communicate underwater using similar clicking noises (Barklow, 1995), as well as having many other behavioural and physiological similarities (Gatesy et al., 1996). But despite this, the most significant line of evidence was the genetic analyses showing the similarity of hippos and cetaceans (such as their milk casein genes) that ultimately settled the case for their close relatedness (Gatesy et al., 1996). But what gives genetics such a privileged role?

In classifying different species, biologists had to routinely learn that the visual similarity between different species, such as birds, is no guarantee of their close relatedness. For instance, the Australian magpie (*Gymnorhina tibicen*) was so named by Europeans due their close similarity in appearance to Eurasian magpies (*Pica pica*), but has turned out not to be closely related at all, not even belonging to the Corvid family. Because of convergent evolution, different species that are only distantly related to each other can exhibit striking parallels in physiology and behaviour. Genetic sequencing studies do not suffer from this ambiguity found in other sources of evidence, providing more objective evidentiary support. While it is important to gather evidence from a variety of sources to test and evaluate models, evidence from molecular genetics can nevertheless often trump other sources of evidence. We can consider it as a kind of gold standard for testing evolutionary models, though this by no means implies that other sources of evidence have become irrelevant.

This point is perhaps the most easily illustrated within the context of palaeontology, which is the study of the fossil record and relies primarily on non-genetic data. Unfortunately, although modern advances in molecular biology have made it possible to gather of some genetic material from fossilized remains (Abdelhady et al., 2024; Briggs et al., 2000; Dobson, 2012; Oskam et al., 2010; Rohland et al., 2018), success is rare and estimated to be restricted to a time horizon of 1.5 million years, due to degradation of DNA strands over time (Kaplan, 2012). Thus, fossilized bones have largely remained as the only remnants of many extinct species.

Consequently, many phylogenetic tree models describing species such as dinosaurs have to rely on the fossil record as the primary line of evidence to support their models. The discovery of feathered dinosaur fossils, for instance, provided increasing support over the years for models that considered birds to have evolved from dinosaurs (Chatterjee, 2015; Chiappe, 2009; G. Mayr, 2016; Rashid et al., 2014; Zhou, 2004). Indeed, because the fossil record is incomplete, new findings often lead to revisions, or indeed to further support for our best hypotheses about the relationships between species.

The location of fossils is also used to gather information about the distribution and migration of species in the past, so it is unsurprising that the study of the distributions of contemporary living species (biogeography) can also be a source of evidence. Additionally, evidence for homologies (similarities) between species can come from embryological and developmental data, anatomical studies, and even behavioural observations and tests (such as the clicking noises made by cetaceans and hippos), to support or undermine hypotheses in tree of life models.

While these data sources are useful for testing phylogenetic models, what about the concrete models we discussed earlier, where evolution itself is simulated in a population, in order to model some other target or a general evolutionary dynamic? Often, these systems are used precisely because no experiment could be run in the target population and thus no data gathered. So how are these models validated? What modellers do in such circumstances is to study the relevant similarities between their model populations and target populations using various sources of data. When they are similar enough for the purposes at hand, that gives us reason to think that our model populations can help us to explain and predict evolutionary patterns in the target population.

In some concrete models designed to examine more theoretical aspects of evolution, such as microbial models of the evolution of multicellularity, there is often no clear target. It is precisely because we do not know how this transition happened, that we use model populations to examine the possible scenarios for *how things might have happened* and to examine the plausibility of alternative scenarios. Recall the earlier distinction between *models for* and *models of*. The latter are assessed in terms of accurate representations, but the same cannot be said for the former (Ratti, 2020). Concrete models in such cases often function very similarly to highly idealized mathematical models that do not have clear biological targets that would allow for traditional empirical tests. Both of these types of models need to rely instead on other methods of testing. Indeed, as we shall now see, such concrete models are tested in a very similar way to mathematical models: theoretically through possibility proofs and robustness analysis.

4.3 Theoretical Tests of Evolution

When one thinks of testing, it will typically be experiments, or at least observational studies, that come to mind. But not all kinds of testing operate in this manner. As was shown in our discussion of concrete models of the evolution of multicellularity, some models do not have a respective target system from which we could derive data to test the models. Some models seem to not be testable through any of these empirical means. This applies especially to mathematical models that are often so highly abstracted and idealized that it becomes hard to see what would even constitute a test.

Maynard Smith's book on models of evolutionary game theory provides a striking example. He makes little reference to actual data and yet the book is considered a founding text for an important subfield of evolutionary biology. Mathematical models and simulations of the evolution of cooperation, for instance, involve so many idealizations in their game-theoretic models that it would be hard to see how they can be tested empirically. Though we know that cooperation has evolved in many lineages, this cannot serve as confirmation for these models, since testing has to happen after a model is created and not before. Indeed, doing the opposite is often considered close to scientific fraud. Scientists who change their models after running experiments, in order to make them better fit the data and/or because their hypothesis was not supported by the results, are often criticized for engaging in 'HARKing: Hypothesizing after the results are known' (N. L. Kerr, 1998). Admittedly, there can be a blurry boundary here between refining models to improve their accuracy and retroactively fitting them to the data for the purposes of publication. One involves retrofitting models while pretending that this was the original form of the model, just to gain a publication. The other makes this refinement process explicit, to allow for transparency.

In our new age of artificial intelligence and machine learning, it will become more and more common to feed vast amounts of empirical data into machine learning algorithms to come up with new predictive and explanatory models, which raises unique scientific and philosophical challenges (Greener et al., 2022). The use of AI and machine learning algorithms to help evolutionary biologists to create better models is only in its infancy (though see Callier, 2022; Feltes et al., 2018; Kuzenkov et al., 2020; Lürig et al., 2021; Tarca et al., 2007), but I am confident that this is an area where the philosophy of models will need to pay a lot of attention in the future. One of the most promising uses of this technology is in training machine learning algorithms to distinguish the effects of drift and selection in shaping changes of the genome of a species (Callier, 2022, p. 2). Nevertheless, while it is worth mentioning these tools here due their plausible future importance, it is currently not yet significant enough to give them more space within the confines of this short Element.

What is significant, however, is that despite the lack of direct empirical confirmation for most models of the evolution of cooperation, scientists continue to create new models and find this activity meaningful. This might seem mysterious if not for the fact that models can receive theoretical support through other models, which is an idea I shall now turn towards:

> [T]he ability of theory to circumvent practical obstructions of experimental tractability in order to tackle virtually any problem is a benefit that should not be underestimated. Science is a quest for knowledge, and if a problem is, at least currently, empirically intractable, it is very unsatisfactory to collectively throw up our hands and accept ignorance. Surely it is far better, in such cases, to use mathematical models to explore how evolution might have proceeded, illuminating the conditions under which certain evolutionary paths are possible. (Servedio et al., 2014, p. 5)

Mathematical models can show us possibilities, as well as allow us to examine how stable/robust the dynamics or effects in our models are. Whether we should really call such theoretical work testing is up for debate. As I mentioned before, in the minds of many, testing implies empirical tests. Ever since Quine's attack on logical positivists in his article 'Two Dogmas of Empiricism' (Quine, 1951), however, the seemingly sharp boundary between analytic statements (true by definition) and synthetic statements (true in virtue of correct descriptions of the world) statements, or theoretical and empirical work, has been contested. The results of theoretical models, just like those from empirical work, can become parts of our network of beliefs. If modellers create a broad range of models with altered assumptions and parameters to show that a particular process or outcome, such as the evolution of cooperation, is robust, then this can strengthen our confidence just as experimental work would. Whether we ultimately call this 'testing' or not, we have to acknowledge that models can be supported through theoretical work. This doesn't deny that empirical tests may still play unique and perhaps more important roles in the scientific validation of models, only that we shouldn't draw too sharp a boundary here between the types of support. As Lloyd notes, a mathematical model is often used 'as a substitute for a real system on which experiments are done' (Lloyd, 1994, p. 9). In this discussion, I have mentioned the idea of robustness analysis a couple of times without going into more detail, but we shall turn to this now.

In an influential 1966 article, titled 'The Strategy of Model Building in Population Biology', Richard Levins brought robustness analysis to the attention of biologists and philosophers of models. He argued that if models 'despite their different assumptions, lead to similar results we have what we can call a robust theorem which is relatively free of the details of the model' (Levins, 1966, p. 423). This was initially puzzling to philosophers of science, who struggled with the idea that models involving idealizations and literal recognized falsehoods could provide us with true insights into reality. Levins described robustness analysis as providing us with truths at 'the intersection of independent lies' (Levins, 1966, p. 423). This sense of testing models no longer considers only single models but moves us towards sets or collectives of models. While a lot of highly idealized models may not by themselves be considered very useful or epistemically insightful, it is when they come together and collectively point at a stable mechanism or prediction that is immune to variations in the assumptions of a model, that they can be considered to be representing something real. But, as I alluded to before, this is no unique feature of mathematical models. Experimental model systems of the evolution of multicellularity are also engaged in changing the conditions within the model to see if they influence the aggregation of individual cells. While these results are typically not robust and often break down fairly quickly, experimental modellers are nevertheless also engaged in robustness analysis. Does this undermine the distinction between theoretical and empirical tests?

Not necessarily, but once again we should highlight that the similarities between the two cases are more important here than the differences between theory and empirical work in modelling. Both concrete and mathematical models are used to explore how-possibly scenarios as well as to examine how robust a result is within one model once we vary the assumptions. Indeed, sometimes robustness analysis involves creating a concrete version of a mathematical model, or vice versa; such as the mathematical models created by Rainey and his collaborators to further explore hypotheses arising from their experimental work (Black et al., 2020). However, some may criticize the idea that this experimental work could constitute robustness analysis since the models differ in kind. This may well be true if we conceive of robustness analysis in a narrow way. As I have argued in an article titled 'Model Pluralism', the epistemic benefits of multiple models go far beyond robustness analysis (Veit, 2020).

It's not an extreme claim that some phenomena may have aspects that are too complex to be understood or explained within a single model. After all, science makes progress through a combination of the many models we discussed in Section 3. Scientists don't restrict themselves only to the use of mathematical models when working to understand the origins of multicellular organisms. They also employ mental models, verbal models, diagrammatic models, and concrete models. We can distinguish this moderate view on the usefulness of a plurality of models from a more radical thesis that I dubbed strong model pluralism: 'For almost any aspect x of phenomenon y, scientists require multiple models to achieve scientific goal z' (Veit, 2020, p. 96). It would be a naive and overly reductive picture of the philosophy of science if we tried to restrict science to the creation of individual model, each corresponding to a particular goal. After all, as we have discussed, mental and verbal models precede the construction of other kinds of models. Similar to how evolutionary biologists think of populations rather than individuals as the centre of their attention, philosophers of modelling need to engage in population thinking, that is, by treating sets of related models as changing populations of models, with particular names of models counterintuitively referring to sets of models rather than just one particular model (Veit, 2020, p. 107).

The analogy to population thinking is, of course, a loose one since such sets of models used for a particular purpose may have no ancestral relationship and may have been independently created. However, I believe that as this metaphor is familiar to evolutionary biologists, it will be helpful in avoiding too much emphasis on individual models. Variation of populations – just like for models – should be the starting point of our investigations. If we talk of the scientific importance of the Hawk–Dove Game, for instance, we do not mean just a particular form of the game, but hundreds of variations of the basic setup. A verbal model that comes to be explicated in precise mathematical form without losing its core argument may be considered at least as a soft confirmation of a theory. And verbal and mental models may be used to check whether slight alterations will significantly change the result of a (fairly simple) model without necessarily requiring it to be modelled mathematically. Scientific articles in evolutionary biology frequently feature sets of models (e.g. concrete, verbal, diagrammatic, and mathematical, see Kerr et al., 2002) of very different types to argue for a particular explanation and we should therefore be careful not to reduce all progress in evolutionary biology only to specific mathematical and concrete models that have undergone tests.

Philosophers of models have only scratched the surface of the ways in which different kinds of models interact with each other to solve epistemological problems, but we can at least attest that we should not prioritize formal models in a sort of hierarchy over more informal models, even when it comes to their testability. As Gunawardena notes, if the assumptions in a formal model 'are at odds with your informal model, then life gets interesting, and you have to decide which to change; formal and informal models ought to work together, each influencing the other in a virtuous cycle; but this may be harder than it looks, if evolutionary biology is any guide' (Gunawardena, 2014, p. 3442). With this in mind let me now summarize this section.

4.4 Summary

This section highlighted many of the ways in which models in evolutionary biology can be tested and yet we have only scratched the surface. Creating testable models is uniquely challenging within evolutionary biology, due to the slow and hidden nature of the processes of interest. As Maynard Smith once put it, 'Evolution is a historical process; it is a unique sequence of events. This raises special difficulties in formulating and testing scientific theories, but I do not think the difficulties are insuperable' (Maynard Smith, 1982, p. 8). As we have seen in this section, evolutionary biologists have come up with many ingenious ways to provide data to test their models. Models are not just products of science, and they also play fundamental roles in scientific practice. As Plutynski argues, 'the diverse types and functions of models and modelling in biology are not easily categorized as either product or process' (Plutynski, 2001, p. 225). However, is the purpose of models in evolutionary biology simply to generate new hypotheses that are then tested through empirical work?

As I have shown here, this is a far too reductive take, with many models being supported through theoretical means such as robustness analysis, as well as through their relationships to whole sets of models more generally. Indeed, while the importance of testing is often emphasized by modellers themselves, they often have very liberal views on what testing consists in. This deflates the notion almost to the extent that we are merely capturing all the methods for evaluating whether a model is good or bad (or at least better than its alternatives). If we restrict the term 'testing' to specific empirical tests of particular hypotheses, we may well want to distinguish it from various forms of data fitting, robustness analysis, and the more general fit of a model with other models. Depending on the particular purpose(s) of a model, we will be interested in different forms of evaluation. Are we interested in explaining the evolution of a particular trait in the real world? Or might we be interested in modelling a fictional trait that has never been observed in the biological world? How general is our model meant to be? All of these questions will change how the model is being evaluated, without there being a general methodological answer for how to proceed. A general model, of cooperation and the evolution of altruism, for instance, can draw on significantly more data than a model restricted to altruism in honeybees. The particular goals of the modeller, as well as context of the problem at hand will determine how models should be tested, and this will almost always lead to the creation of further models.

5 Conclusion and Further Discussion

This Element concerned three broad themes. Firstly, what it means to be a 'model' and what it means to engage in 'modelling'? Secondly, what types of models are there in evolutionary biology? Thirdly, I examined the question of how models of evolution can be tested? While this Element hopes to have made progress on all of these questions, many puzzles remain. I hope that philosophers of models, philosophers of biology, and evolutionary biologists get away from this Element with an appreciation for the richness and difficulties in the philosophy of modelling evolution, and perhaps the motivation to contribute to this literature themselves. Some readers may have hoped that philosophers have settled all these questions conclusively and that this Element would simply serve as a summary of the conclusions philosophers of modelling have arrived at. But philosophy unfortunately rarely leads to such simple progress. Often, we investigate a problem only to learn that it is even more complex than we might have anticipated. Frequently, I was only able to scratch the surface of further questions that arise from a philosophical examination of these questions, but I hope that this only emphasizes how rich this literature is and how much work has to be done. Nevertheless, I hope that I have succeeded in showing that progress in our understanding of 'models' and 'modelling' in evolutionary biology can be made.

One central idea in understanding models was the notion of representations. There is a broad consensus that it is useful to understand models as representations of a particular target system for a certain purpose. For instance, as is common in evolutionary biology, we might be interested in investigating a kind of placeholder system, such as microbial population models of evolutionary dynamics, or to summarize data as in phylogenetic tree models for the purposes of education. Crucially, it is the goal of the modeller here that matters for considerations of whether a model succeeds or not – there is no independent model evaluation from that. However, once we examine the purposes of models in more detail the representationalist view of models appears on shaky ground. Firstly, it is too broad to capture a unique scientific category. Secondly, the view is too narrow and misses out on a plurality of other ways in which models are used in science that have little to do with their representational roles, such as models for interventions. We also considered the radical thesis of *model anarchism*, that what we call 'models' and 'modelling' is simply too broad, capturing too many different things, as that a unifying philosophical account could be given. But even with the possibility that these terms may just reflect sociological facts about how scientists decide to call particular scientific tools conditional on their discipline and field, it is nevertheless a useful framework to think of many models used by evolutionary biologists as representations for specific targets. Where the goals of models deviate from this we will need to examine the cases more carefully, but it remains a useful approximation.

From phylogenetic trees, model populations, and thought experiments, to game-theoretic models, there is an incredible wealth of representationalist devices that have been developed to not only advance the scientific understanding of evolution, but also to convince the public of the truth of Darwin's theory of evolution by natural selection. That there is a plurality of ways in which evolution can be modelled has admittedly been recognized as early as 1983, when Maynard Smith made 'a plea for pluralism in the ways in which we model evolution' in an article fittingly titled *Models of Evolution* (Maynard Smith, 1983, p. 315). By this he largely meant the assumptions, idealizations, and omissions that go into mathematical models of evolution. But as I hope to have shown in this Element, there are many different types of models evolutionary biologists can employ to advance our understanding of evolution. Mental models stand at the beginning of much scientific theorizing as the most informal kind of model. Just like verbal and linguistic models, their background assumptions are often implicit, but may come to the forefront in discussions with others or in trying to spell them out in writing. Evolutionary biology is full of diagrammatic and pictorial models representing ancestral relationships and species that are long extinct, which are not only used in education, but as crucial tools of scientific reasoning in scientific publications, which have come a long way from simple drawings by hand. We also discussed concrete models which can help us to study evolution directly in the lab. Finally, we discussed mathematical, computational, and statistical models, as the most formal types of models there are, with a kind of precision other types of models lack. This typology was not hierarchical but simply meant to order models from the least formal to the most formal. They have their unique benefits and drawbacks, which need to be carefully considered depending on the goals of the modeller.

Next, we discussed the many forms models can be 'tested' in practice, which requires a careful examination of the particular purpose(s) of the model. Tests are often empirical in nature, drawing on many different areas such as the fossil record and physiological studies, but I also emphasized the important role of theoretical tests to examine how-possibly scenarios within evolutionary biology and robustness tests of models to examine how stable these results are even with changing assumptions. Yet, some models such as model populations for the study of multicellularity blur the boundary between theory and practice also relying on robustness tests for their how-possibly explanations. We also learned that models typically work in tandem with other models more generally and that much work remains to be done for philosophers of modelling to uncover how different types of models interact with each other. A diversity of different forms of evidence will often be what we are after, but evolutionary biology also gives special priority to genetic evidence from molecular biology due to its reliability and historical record-keeping.

At the beginning of this Element, I set out my goal to write an interesting synthesis of the philosophy of models and evolutionary biology that would appeal to philosophers of modelling, philosophers of biology, and evolutionary biologists. But writing an introduction for distinct audiences brings unique challenges. For philosophers of science and modelling my discussion will perhaps seem pitched at too low a level, whereas evolutionary biologists may consider some of the material too philosophical. I hope to have found a good mid-way point between these audiences that emphasizes (i) how philosophers of modelling can learn much from the unique modelling strategies in evolutionary biology and (ii) how evolutionary biologists can use the insights from the philosophy of models to inform their own modelling practice and theorizing. Evolutionary biology is full of rich case studies that deserve much more detailed treatment by philosophers than I was able to offer here and that should entertain them for the decades to come. Conversely, evolutionary biologists will benefit from studying the philosophy of models literature on specific modelling goals depending on what they are currently aiming to achieve. For philosophers of biology this Element should have made clear that we need to pay more attention to the models employed by evolutionary biologists to make progress in the field I also hope that this Element will enable future collaborations between philosophers and evolutionary biologists to make progress on many of the unsettled questions I have raised here. But all of these more ambitious hopes aside, I simply hope that my readers have enjoyed this Element on modelling evolution.

References

Abdelhady, A. A., Seuss, B., Jain, S., Fathy, D., Sami, M., Ali, A., Elsheikh, A., Ahmed, M. S., Elewa, A. M., & Hussain, A. M. (2024). Molecular technology in paleontology and paleobiology: Applications and limitations. *Quaternary International*, 685, 24–38.

Abenes, F. M. D., & Caballes, D. G. (2020). Misconceptions of science teachers in evolution. *Biometrics and Bioinformatics*, 12(2), 31–38.

Aguirre-Liguori, J. A., Ramírez-Barahona, S., & Gaut, B. S. (2021). The evolutionary genomics of species' responses to climate change. *Nature Ecology & Evolution*, 5(10), 1350–1360.

Ankeny, R., & Leonelli, S. (2020). *Model Organisms* (1st ed.). Cambridge University Press. https://doi.org/10.1017/9781108593014

Barklow, W. (1995). Hippo talk. *Natural History*, 104(5), 54

Bergstrom, C. T., & Dugatkin, L. A. (2012). *Evolution* (1st ed.). Norton.

Black, A. J., Bourrat, P., & Rainey, P. B. (2020). Ecological scaffolding and the evolution of individuality. *Nature Ecology & Evolution*, 4(3), 426–436. https://doi.org/10.1038/s41559-019-1086-9

Bokulich, A. (2014). How the tiger bush got its stripes: 'how possibly' vs. 'how actually' model explanations. *The Monist*, 97(3), 321–338.

Bolker, J. A. (2009). Exemplary and surrogate models: Two modes of representation in biology. *Perspectives in Biology and Medicine*, 52(4), 485–499.

Bourrat, P. (2021). *Facts, Conventions, and the Levels of Selection*. Cambridge University Press. www.cambridge.org/core/elements/facts-conventions-and-the-levels-of-selection/8EAF88974A3BE92761217A2EC6AB4634

Bourrat, P., Takacs, P., Doulcier, G., Nitschke, M. C., Black, A. J., Hammerschmidt, K., & Rainey, P. B. (2024). Individuality through ecology: Rethinking the evolution of complex life from an externalist perspective. *Ecology and Evolution*, 14(12), e70661. https://doi.org/10.1002/ece3.70661

Briggs, D. E., Evershed, R. P., & Lockheart, M. J. (2000). The biomolecular paleontology of continental fossils. *Paleobiology*, 26(S4), 169–193.

Brown, J. M., & Thomson, R. C. (2018). Evaluating model performance in evolutionary biology. *Annual Review of Ecology, Evolution, and Systematics*, 49(1), 95–114. https://doi.org/10.1146/annurev-ecolsys-110617-062249

Callender, C., & Cohen, J. (2006). There is no special problem about scientific representation. *THEORIA*, 21(1), 67–85. https://doi.org/10.1387/theoria.554

Callier, V. (2022). Machine learning in evolutionary studies comes of age. *Proceedings of the National Academy of Sciences*, 119(17), e2205058119. https://doi.org/10.1073/pnas.2205058119

Chatterjee, S. (2015). *The Rise of Birds: 225 million years of Evolution*. JHU Press. https://books.google.com/books?hl=en&lr=&id=V-okBwAAQBAJ&oi=fnd&pg=PP1&dq=dinosaur+bird+evolution+fossil&ots=wIw3fOPC8T&sig=gekQsE8UMJHuKPZYjLDj8BVLrlg

Chiappe, L. M. (2009). Downsized Dinosaurs: The evolutionary transition to modern birds. *Evolution: Education and Outreach*, 2(2), 248–256. https://doi.org/10.1007/s12052-009-0133-4

Chown, S. L., Hoffmann, A. A., Kristensen, T. N., AngillettaJr, M. J., Stenseth, N. C., & Pertoldi, C. (2010). Adapting to climate change: A perspective from evolutionary physiology. *Climate Research*, 43(1–2), 3–15.

Cotner, S., & Wassenberg, D. (2020). *The evolution and biology of sex*. Available through the University of Minnesota Affordable Content Partnership. https://open.lib.umn.edu/evolutionbiology/

d'Apollonia, S. T., Charles, Elizabeth S., & Boyd, G. M. (2004). Acquisition of complex systemic thinking: Mental models of evolution. *Educational Research and Evaluation*, 10(4–6), 499–521. https://doi.org/10.1080/13803610512331383539

Darwin, C. (1837). *Notebooks on Transmutation of Species* (p. 36). https://darwin-online.org.uk/content/frameset?itemID=CUL-DAR121.-&viewtype=image&pageseq=1.

Darwin, C. (1859). *On the Origin of Species by Means of Natural Selection, or the Preservation of Favoured Races in the Struggle for Life*. John Murray.

de Oliveira, G. S. (2021). Representationalism is a dead end. *Synthese*, 198(1), 209–235. https://doi.org/10.1007/s11229-018-01995-9

De Santis, M. D. (2021). Misconceptions about historical sciences in evolutionary biology. *Evolutionary Biology*, 48(1), 94–99. https://doi.org/10.1007/s11692-020-09526-6

Dimech, D. K. (2017). Modelling with words: Narrative and natural selection. *Studies in History and Philosophy of Science Part C: Studies in History and Philosophy of Biological and Biomedical Sciences*, 62, 20–24. https://doi.org/10.1016/j.shpsc.2017.02.003

Dobson, E. (2012). *Search for Ancient DNA, the Meaning of Fossils, and Paleontology in the Modern Evolutionary Synthesis*. https://repository.lib.fsu.edu/islandora/object/fsu:182834

Downes, S. M. (2011). Scientific models. *Philosophy Compass*, 6(11), 757–764. https://doi.org/10.1111/j.1747-9991.2011.00441.x

Downes, S. M. (2020). *Models and Modeling in the Sciences: A Philosophical Introduction* (1st ed.). Routledge. https://doi.org/10.4324/9781315647456

Elgin, M., & Sober, E. (2017). Popper's shifting appraisal of evolutionary theory. *HOPOS: The Journal of the International Society for the History of Philosophy of Science*, 7(1), 31–55. https://doi.org/10.1086/691119

Feltes, B. C., Grisci, B. I., de Faria Poloni, J., & Dorn, M. (2018). Perspectives and applications of machine learning for evolutionary developmental biology. *Molecular Omics*, 14(5), 289–306.

Friedman, M. (1953). The methodology of positive economics. In M. Friedman (ed.), *Essays in Positive Economics* (pp. 3–43). University of Chicago Press.

Frigg, R. (2022). *Models and Theories: A Philosophical Inquiry* (1st ed.). Routledge. https://doi.org/10.4324/9781003285106

Frigg, R., & Nguyen, J. (2016). The fiction view of models reloaded. *The Monist*, 99(3), 225–242. https://doi.org/10.1093/monist/onw002

Frigg, R., & Nguyen, J. (2017). Models and representation. In L. Magnani, & T. Bertolotti (eds.), *Springer Handbook of Model-Based Science* (pp. 49–102). Springer International Publishing. https://doi.org/10.1007/978-3-319-30526-4_3

Frigg, R., & Nguyen, J. (2021). Scientific representation. In E. N. Zalta (ed.), *The Stanford Encyclopedia of Philosophy* (Winter 2021). Metaphysics Research Lab, Stanford University. https://plato.stanford.edu/archives/win2021/entries/scientific-representation/

Futuyma, D. J. (2006). *Evolutionary Biology*. W.H. Freeman.

Gatesy, J., Hayashi, C., Cronin, M. A., & Arctander, P. (1996). Evidence from milk casein genes that cetaceans are close relatives of hippopotamid artiodactyls. *Molecular Biology and Evolution*, 13(7), 954–963. https://doi.org/10.1093/oxfordjournals.molbev.a025663

Gelfert, A. (2019). Probing possibilities: Toy models, minimal models, and exploratory models. In Á. Nepomuceno-Fernández, L. Magnani, F. J. Salguero-Lamillar, C. Barés-Gómez, & M. Fontaine (eds.), *Model-Based Reasoning in Science and Technology* (Vol. 49, pp. 3–19). Springer International Publishing. https://doi.org/10.1007/978-3-030-32722-4_1

Gibbons, A. (2012). Bonobos join chimps as closest human relatives. *Science*, 13. https://doi.org/10.1126/article.25670

Giere, R. N. (1988). *Explaining Science: A Cognitive Approach*. University of Chicago Press.

Giere, R. N. (2001). The nature and function of models. *Behavioral and Brain Sciences*, 24(6), 1060–1060.

Godfrey-Smith, P. (2007). The strategy of model-based science. *Biology & Philosophy*, 21(5), 725–740. https://doi.org/10.1007/s10539-006-9054-6

Goodman, N. (1976). *Languages of Art: An Approach to a Theory of Symbols* (2nd ed., [Nachdr.]). Hackett.

Gould, S. J. (1990). *Wonderful Life: The Burgess Shale and the Nature of History* (1st ed.). W. W. Norton & Company, Incorporated.

Greener, J. G., Kandathil, S. M., Moffat, L., & Jones, D. T. (2022). A guide to machine learning for biologists. *Nature Reviews Molecular Cell Biology*, 23(1), 40–55. https://doi.org/10.1038/s41580-021-00407-0

Gregory, T. R. (2008). Understanding evolutionary trees. *Evolution: Education and Outreach*, 1(2), 121–137. https://doi.org/10.1007/s12052-008-0035-x

Gregory, T. R. (2009). Understanding natural selection: Essential concepts and common misconceptions. *Evolution: Education and Outreach*, 2(2), 156–175. https://doi.org/10.1007/s12052-009-0128-1

Griesemer, J. R. (1990). Material models in biology. *PSA: Proceedings of the Biennial Meeting of the Philosophy of Science Association*, 1990(2), 79–93. https://doi.org/10.1086/psaprocbienmeetp.1990.2.193060

Gunawardena, J. (2014). Beware the tail that wags the dog: Informal and formal models in biology. *Molecular Biology of the Cell*, 25(22), 3441–3444. https://doi.org/10.1091/mbc.e14-02-0717

Hammerschmidt, K., Rose, C. J., Kerr, B., & Rainey, P. B. (2014). Life cycles, fitness decoupling and the evolution of multicellularity. *Nature*, 515(7525), 75.

Hinchliff, C. E., Smith, S. A., Allman, J. F., Burleigh, J. G., Chaudhary, R., Coghill, L. M., Crandall, K. A., Deng, J., Drew, B. T., Gazis, R., Gude, K., Hibbett, D. S., Katz, L. A., Laughinghouse, H. D., McTavish, E. J., Midford, P. E., Owen, C. L., Ree, R. H., Rees, J. A., ... Cranston, K. A. (2015). Synthesis of phylogeny and taxonomy into a comprehensive tree of life. *Proceedings of the National Academy of Sciences*, 112(41), 12764–12769. https://doi.org/10.1073/pnas.1423041112

Hughes, R. I. G. (1997). Models and representation. *Philosophy of Science*, 64(S4), S325–S336. https://doi.org/10.1086/392611

Kaplan, M. (2012). DNA has a 521-year half-life. *Nature.* https://doi.org/10.1038/nature.2012.11555

Keller, E. F. (2000). Models of and models for: Theory and practice in contemporary biology. *Philosophy of Science*, 67, S72–S86.

Kerr, B., Riley, M. A., Feldman, M. W., & Bohannan, B. J. (2002). Local dispersal promotes biodiversity in a real-life game of rock–paper–scissors. *Nature*, 418(6894), 171.

Kerr, N. L. (1998). HARKing: Hypothesizing after the results are known. *Personality and Social Psychology Review*, 2(3), 196–217. https://doi.org/10.1207/s15327957pspr0203_4

Kuzenkov, O., Morozov, A., & Kuzenkova, G. (2020). Exploring evolutionary fitness in biological systems using machine learning methods. *Entropy*, 23(1), 35.

Levins, R. (1966). The strategy of model building in population biology. *American Scientist*, 54(4), 421–431.

Lewens, T. (2024). *Cultural Selection.* Cambridge University Press.

Lloyd, E. A. (1994). *The Structure and Confirmation of Evolutionary Theory* (1. Princeton paperback print). Princeton University Press.

Loughney, K. M., Badgley, C., Bahadori, A., Holt, W. E., & Rasbury, E. T. (2021). Tectonic influence on Cenozoic mammal richness and sedimentation history of the Basin and Range, western North America. *Science Advances*, 7(45), eabh4470. https://doi.org/10.1126/sciadv.abh4470

Lürig, M. D., Donoughe, S., Svensson, E. I., Porto, A., & Tsuboi, M. (2021). Computer vision, machine learning, and the promise of phenomics in ecology and evolutionary biology. *Frontiers in Ecology and Evolution*, 9, 642774.

Mäki, U. (2009). MISSing the world. Models as isolations and credible surrogate systems. *Erkenntnis*, 70(1), 29–43.

Massimi, M. (2019). Two kinds of exploratory models. *Philosophy of Science*, 86(5), 869–881.

Maynard Smith, J. (1982). *Evolution and the Theory of Games.* Cambridge University Press.

Maynard Smith, J. (1983). Models of evolution. *Proceedings of the Royal Society of London. Series B. Biological Sciences*, 219(1216), 315–325. https://doi.org/10.1098/rspb.1983.0076

Maynard Smith, J., & Price, G. R. (1973). The logic of animal conflict. *Nature*, 246(5427), 15–18. https://doi.org/10.1038/246015a0

Mayr, E. (1982). *The Growth of Biological Thought.* Harvard University Press.

Mayr, E. (1983). How to carry out the adaptationist program? *The American Naturalist*, 121(3), 324–334. https://doi.org/10.1086/284064

Mayr, G. (2016). *Avian Evolution: The Fossil Record of Birds and Its Paleobiological Significance*. John Wiley & Sons. https://books.google.com/books?hl=en&lr=&id=UNqTDgAAQBAJ&oi=fnd&pg=PP13&dq=dinosaur+bird+evolution+fossil&ots=q_ssRP0Hez&sig=Q-TrLGjqYJ1qsvQcDnFGrJj9CFU

McGlothlin, J. W., Akçay, E., Brodie, E. D., III, Moore, A. J., & Van Cleve, J. (2022). A Synthesis of game theory and quantitative genetic models of social evolution. *Journal of Heredity*, 113(1), 109–119. https://doi.org/10.1093/jhered/esab064

Meir, E., Perry, J., Herron, J. C., & Kingsolver, J. (2007). College students' misconceptions about evolutionary trees. *The American Biology Teacher*, 69(7). https://bioone.org/journals/the-american-biology-teacher/volume-69/issue-7/0002-7685(2007)69[71:CSMAET]2.0.CO;2/College-Students-Misconceptions-About-Evolutionary-Trees/10.1662/0002-7685(2007)69[71:CSMAET]2.0.CO;2.full

Mitchell, M. W., & Gonder, M. K. (2013). Primate speciation: A case study of African apes. *Nature Education Knowledge*, 4(2), 1.

Moody, E. R. R., Álvarez-Carretero, S., Mahendrarajah, T. A., Clark, J. W., Betts, H. C., Dombrowski, N., Szánthó, L. L., Boyle, R. A., Daines, S., Chen, X., Lane, N., Yang, Z., Shields, G. A., Szöllősi, G. J., Spang, A., Pisani, D., Williams, T. A., Lenton, T. M., & Donoghue, P. C. J. (2024). The nature of the last universal common ancestor and its impact on the early Earth system. *Nature Ecology & Evolution*, 8(9), 1654–1666. https://doi.org/10.1038/s41559-024-02461-1

Mueller, L. D., & Joshi, A. (2000). *Stability in Model Populations*. Princeton University Press.

Munday, P. L., Warner, R. R., Monro, K., Pandolfi, J. M., & Marshall, D. J. (2013). Predicting evolutionary responses to climate change in the sea. *Ecology Letters*, 16(12), 1488–1500. https://doi.org/10.1111/ele.12185

Myin, E., & Hutto, D. D. (2015). REC: Just radical enough. *Studies in Logic, Grammar and Rhetoric*, 41(1), 61–71.

Nehm, R. H., & Reilly, L. (2007). Biology majors' knowledge and misconceptions of natural selection. *BioScience*, 57(3), 263–272.

Nehm, R. H., Poole, T. M., Lyford, M. E., Hoskins, S. G., Carruth, L., Ewers, B. E., & Colberg, P. J. S. (2009). Does the segregation of evolution in biology textbooks and introductory courses reinforce students' faulty mental models of biology and evolution? *Evolution: Education and Outreach*, 2(3), 527–532. https://doi.org/10.1007/s12052-008-0100-5

Nelson, C. E. (2008). Teaching evolution (and all of biology) more effectively: Strategies for engagement, critical reasoning, and confronting misconceptions. *American Zoologist*, 48(2), 213–225.

Neto, C., Meynell, L., & Jones, C. T. (2023). Scaffolds and scaffolding: An explanatory strategy in evolutionary biology. *Biology & Philosophy*, 38(2), 8. https://doi.org/10.1007/s10539-023-09897-y

Nguyen, J., & Frigg, R. (2022). Maps, models, and representation. In I. Lawler, K. Khalifa, & E. Shech (eds.), *Scientific Understanding and Representation* (pp. 261–279). Routledge.

Nikaido, M., Rooney, A. P., & Okada, N. (1999). Phylogenetic relationships among cetartiodactyls based on insertions of short and long interpersed elements: Hippopotamuses are the closest extant relatives of whales. *Proceedings of the National Academy of Sciences of the United States of America*, 96(18), 10261. https://doi.org/10.1073/pnas.96.18.10261

O'Connor, C., & Weatherall, J. O. (2016). Black Holes, Black-Scholes, and Prairie Voles: An essay review of simulation and similarity, by Michael Weisberg. *Philosophy of Science*, 83(4), 613–626.

Odenbaugh, J. (2018). Models, models, models: A deflationary view. *Synthese*. https://doi.org/10.1007/s11229-017-1665-8

Odenbaugh, J. (2019). *Ecological Models* (1st ed.). Cambridge University Press. https://doi.org/10.1017/9781108685283

O'Malley, M. A., & Koonin, E. V. (2011). How stands the Tree of Life a century and a half after The Origin? *Biology Direct*, 6(1), 32. https://doi.org/10.1186/1745-6150-6-32

O'Malley, M. A., Travisano, M., Velicer, G. J., & Bolker, J. A. (2015). How do microbial populations and communities function as model systems? *The Quarterly Review of Biology*, 90(3), 269–293. https://doi.org/10.1086/682588

Oskam, C. L., Haile, J., McLay, E., Rigby, P., Allentoft, M. E., Olsen, M. E., Bengtsson, C., Miller, G. H., Schwenninger, J.-L., Jacomb, C., Walter, R., Baynes, A., Dortch, J., Parker-Pearson, M., Gilbert, M. T. P., Holdaway, R. N., Willerslev, E., & Bunce, M. (2010). Fossil avian eggshell preserves ancient DNA. *Proceedings of the Royal Society B: Biological Sciences*, 277(1690), 1991–2000. https://doi.org/10.1098/rspb.2009.2019

Otsuka, J. (2019). *The Role of Mathematics in Evolutionary Theory* (1st ed.). Cambridge University Press. https://doi.org/10.1017/9781108672115

Oxford English Dictionary. (2024). model, n. & adj. Oxford University Press; Oxford English Dictionary. https://doi.org/10.1093/OED/3984201854

Parker, W. S. (2020). Model evaluation: An adequacy-for-purpose view. *Philosophy of Science*, 87(3), 457–477.

Pau, S., Wolkovich, E. M., Cook, B. I., Davies, T. J., Kraft, N. J. B., Bolmgren, K., Betancourt, J. L., & Cleland, E. E. (2011). Predicting phenology by integrating ecology, evolution and climate science. *Global Change Biology*, 17(12), 3633–3643. https://doi.org/10.1111/j.1365-2486.2011.02515.x

Plutynski, A. (2001). Modeling evolution in theory and practice. *Philosophy of Science*, 68(S3), S225–S236. https://doi.org/10.1086/392911

Popper, K. (1957). *The Poverty of Historicism*. Routledge & Kegan Paul. www.taylorfrancis.com/books/mono/10.4324/9780203538012/poverty-historicism-karl-popper

Popper, K. (1978). Natural selection and the emergence of mind. *Dialectica*, 32(3–4), 339–355. https://doi.org/10.1111/j.1746-8361.1978.tb01321.x

Potochnik, A. (2017). *Idealization and the Aims of Science*. University of Chicago Press.

Prüfer, K., Munch, K., Hellmann, I., Akagi, K., Miller, J. R., Walenz, B., Koren, S., Sutton, G., Kodira, C., Winer, R., Knight, J. R., Mullikin, J. C., Meader, S. J., Ponting, C. P., Lunter, G., Higashino, S., Hobolth, A., Dutheil, J., Karakoç, E., ... Pääbo, S. (2012). The bonobo genome compared with the chimpanzee and human genomes. *Nature*, 486(7404), 527–531. https://doi.org/10.1038/nature11128

Quine, W. V. O. (1951). Two Dogmas of empiricism. *PR*, 60, 20–43.

Rashid, D. J., Chapman, S. C., Larsson, H. C., Organ, C. L., Bebin, A.-G., Merzdorf, C. S., Bradley, R., & Horner, J. R. (2014). From dinosaurs to birds: A tail of evolution. *EvoDevo*, 5(1), 25. https://doi.org/10.1186/2041-9139-5-25

Ratti, E. (2020). 'Models of' and 'Models for': On the relation between mechanistic models and experimental strategies in molecular biology. *The British Journal for the Philosophy of Science*, 71(2), 773–797.

Resnik, D. B. (1991). How-possibly explanations in biology. *Acta Biotheoretica*, 39(2), 141–149. https://doi.org/10.1007/BF00046596

Rogers, K. (2023). Scientific modeling. In *Encyclopædia Britannica*. www.britannica.com/science/scientific-modeling

Rohland, N., Glocke, I., Aximu-Petri, A., & Meyer, M. (2018). Extraction of highly degraded DNA from ancient bones, teeth and sediments for high-throughput sequencing. *Nature Protocols*, 13(11), 2447–2461. https://doi.org/10.1038/s41596-018-0050-5

Romeijn, J.-W. (2022). Philosophy of statistics. In E. N. Zalta, & U. Nodelman (eds.), *The Stanford Encyclopedia of Philosophy*

(Fall 2022). Metaphysics Research Lab, Stanford University. https://plato.stanford.edu/archives/fall2022/entries/statistics/

Rose, C. J., Hammerschmidt, K., Pichugin, Y., & Rainey, P. B. (2020). Meta-population structure and the evolutionary transition to multi-cellularity. *Ecology Letters*, 23(9), 1380–1390.

Rosenberg, A. (2009). If economics is a science, what kind of a science is it? In D. Ross, & H. Kincaid (eds.), *The Oxford Handbook of Philosophy of Economics* (pp. 55–67). Oxford University Press.

Rosindell, J., & Harmon, L. J. (2012). *OneZoom: A fractal explorer for the tree of life*. https://journals.plos.org/plosbiology/article?id=10.1371/journal.pbio.1001406

Sack, J. D. (2018). *OneZoom Tree of Life Explorer*. University of California Press USA. https://online.ucpress.edu/abt/article-abstract/80/3/248/19086

Servedio, M. R., Brandvain, Y., Dhole, S., Fitzpatrick, C. L., Goldberg, E. E., Stern, C. A., Van Cleve, J., & Yeh, D. J. (2014). Not just a theory – The utility of mathematical models in evolutionary biology. *PLoS Biology*, 12(12), e1002017. https://doi.org/10.1371/journal.pbio.1002017

Sober, E. (2008). *Evidence and Evolution: The Logic Behind the Science*. Cambridge University Press.

Sonleitner, F. J. (1986). What did Karl Popper really say about Evolution? *Creation/Evolution*, 18, 9–14.

Stamos, D. N. (1996). Popper, falsifiability, and evolutionary biology. *Biology & Philosophy*, 11(2), 161–191. https://doi.org/10.1007/BF00128918

Tarca, A. L., Carey, V. J., Chen, X., Romero, R., & Drăghici, S. (2007). Machine learning and its applications to biology. *PLoS Computational Biology*, 3(6), e116.

Teller, P. (2001). Twilight of the perfect model model. *Erkenntnis (1975-)*, 55(3), 393–415.

The Economist. (2006). A heavyweight champ, at five foot two. *The Economist*. www.economist.com/special-report/2006/11/23/a-heavyweight-champ-at-five-foot-two

Thomson, K. (2017, February 6). Darwin's Literary Models. *American Scientist*. https://www.americanscientist.org/article/darwins-literary-models

Veit, W. (2019a). Modeling morality. In M. Fontaine, C. Barés-Gómez, F. Salguero-Lamillar, L. Magnani, & Á. Nepomuceno-Fernández (eds.), *Model-Based Reasoning in Science and Technology: Inferential*

Models for Logic, Language, Cognition and Computation (pp. 83–102). Springer Verlag.

Veit, W. (2019b). Evolution of multicellularity: Cheating done right. *Biology & Philosophy*, 34(3), 34. https://doi.org/10.1007/s10539-019-9688-9

Veit, W. (2020). Model pluralism. *Philosophy of the Social Sciences*, 50(2), 91–114. https://doi.org/10.1177/0048393119894897

Veit, W. (2022). Scaffolding natural selection. *Biological Theory*, 17(2), 163–180.

Veit, W. (2023). Model anarchism. *Theoria: Revista de Teoría, Historia y Fundamentos de La Ciencia*, 38(2), 225–245.

Veit, W., & Milan, N. (2021). Metaphors in arts and science. *European Journal for Philosophy of Science*, 11(2), 1–24.

Waldvogel, A.-M., Feldmeyer, B., Rolshausen, G., Exposito-Alonso, M., Rellstab, C., Kofler, R., Mock, T., Schmid, K., Schmitt, I., & Bataillon, T. (2020). Evolutionary genomics can improve prediction of species' responses to climate change. *Evolution Letters*, 4(1), 4–18.

Weibull, J. W. (1995). *Evolutionary Game Theory*. MIT Press.

Weisberg, M. (2013). *Simulation and Similarity: Using Models to Understand the World*. Oxford University Press.

Wilensky, U. (2002). NetLogo Models Library: Prisoner's Dilemma Basic Evolutionary. Center for Connected Learning and Computer-Based Modeling, Northwestern University, Evanston, IL. https://ccl.northwestern.edu/netlogo/models/Prisoner'sDilemmaBasicEvolutionary

Wong, Y., & Rosindell, J. (2022). Dynamic visualisation of million-tip trees: The OneZoom project. *Methods in Ecology and Evolution*, 13(2), 303–313. https://doi.org/10.1111/2041-210X.13766

Wortel, M. T., Agashe, D., Bailey, S. F., Bank, C., Bisschop, K., Blankers, T., Cairns, J., Colizzi, E. S., Cusseddu, D., Desai, M. M., Van Dijk, B., Egas, M., Ellers, J., Groot, A. T., Heckel, D. G., Johnson, M. L., Kraaijeveld, K., Krug, J., Laan, L., … Pennings, P. S. (2023). Towards evolutionary predictions: Current promises and challenges. *Evolutionary Applications*, 16(1), 3–21. https://doi.org/10.1111/eva.13513

Yagan, O., Sridhar, A., Eletreby, R., Levin, S., Plotkin, J. B., & Poor, H. V. (2021). Modeling and analysis of the spread of COVID-19 under a multiple-strain model with mutations. *Harvard Data Science Review*, 4. https://assets.pubpub.org/r380a9bz/a11bf693-b0b1-43f7-bc28-77b9ee948797.pdf

Zhou, Z. (2004). The origin and early evolution of birds: Discoveries, disputes, and perspectives from fossil evidence. *Naturwissenschaften*, 91(10), 455–471. https://doi.org/10.1007/s00114-004-0570-4

Acknowledgements

This Element is the result of several years of thinking about evolution, not only within the confines of philosophy, but also in close contact with biologists. During my undergraduate I visited Chaitanya Gokhale's Theoretical models of Eco-evolutionary Dynamics research group at the Max Planck Institute for Evolutionary Biology, and parts of my PhD and post-doc were spent at Roberto Salguero-Gómez's SalGo Team at the Department of Zoology (later the Department of Biology) at the University of Oxford, giving me a first-hand experience of the modelling activities of evolutionary biologists. I thank them for giving me these opportunities that shaped much of my outlook in this Element.

Back in 2019 my goal was to write a PhD thesis on the connection between models and evolutionary biology and while my topic shifted towards the evolution of consciousness this Element gave me the wonderful opportunity to return to this topic in depth. I would also like to thank the series editors Michael Ruse (who unfortunately died in 2024) and Grant Ramsey for giving me this opportunity and their support in bringing this book to fruition. Further thanks go out to Erola Fenollosa who created Figure 2 for this Element.

My sincere thanks go out to Jeremy Gunawardena, Roman Frigg, Greg Currie, David Oderberg, and two anonymous reviewers, for providing me with comments on the manuscript. I would also like to thank my wife Heather Browning for her many comments and copyedits on this manuscript, as well as her love and support. I am responsible for any remaining errors. This Element was supported through Samir Okasha's Representing Evolution project that has received funding from the European Research Council (ERC) under the European Union's Horizon 2020 research and innovation programme (Grant No. 101018533).

Finally, I dedicate this book to John Maynard Smith, who was a pioneer not only in using models in evolutionary biology but also in engaging with philosophers of science. It is largely because of his work that I came in contact with evolutionary game theory during my undergraduate degree in philosophy and economics, which turned my attention towards research in biology more broadly.

I declare that there are no conflicts of interest to report.

Cambridge Elements =

Philosophy of Biology

Grant Ramsey
KU Leuven

Grant Ramsey is a BOFZAP research professor at the Institute of Philosophy, KU Leuven, Belgium. His work centers on philosophical problems at the foundation of evolutionary biology. He has been awarded the Popper Prize twice for his work in this area. He also publishes in the philosophy of animal behavior, human nature and the moral emotions. He runs the Ramsey Lab (theramseylab.org), a highly collaborative research group focused on issues in the philosophy of the life sciences.

About the Series

This Cambridge Elements series provides concise and structured introductions to all of the central topics in the philosophy of biology. Contributors to the series are cutting-edge researchers who offer balanced, comprehensive coverage of multiple perspectives, while also developing new ideas and arguments from a unique viewpoint.

Cambridge Elements

Philosophy of Biology

Elements in the Series

Animal Models of Human Disease
Sara Green

Cultural Selection
Tim Lewens

Biological Organization
Leonardo Bich

Controlled Experiments
Jutta Schickore

Slime Mould and Philosophy
Matthew Sims

Explanation in Biology
Lauren N. Ross

Philosophy of Physiology
Maël Lemoine

The Organism
Jan Baedke

Human Cognitive Diversity
Ingo Brigandt

The Scope of Evolutionary Thinking
Thomas A. C. Reydon

What Is Life? Revisited
Daniel J. Nicholson

Modelling Evolution
Walter Veit

A full series listing is available at: www.cambridge.org/EPBY

For EU product safety concerns, contact us at Calle de José Abascal, 56–1°, 28003 Madrid, Spain or eugpsr@cambridge.org.

www.ingramcontent.com/pod-product-compliance
Lightning Source LLC
LaVergne TN
LVHW011858060526
838200LV00054B/4396